Healing

Out

"I did it, YOU can Too!"

Gillian Bowles MBA

Published by Heartfelt Publications

Terms of Use

Disclaimer

Dedication

I dedicate this book to everyone who has contributed to my own healing journey whether they know it or not.

Index

Introduction

I am here to tell you that you can heal your body naturally without medical intervention.

So who am I to tell you that?

I am a certified Healing Breath-work Practitioner, a Management Consultant with a master's degree and I have been certified by Louise L. Hay to run "You Can Heal Your Life" workshops since 1999. But what really qualifies me to tell you this is the fact that I healed my body quite naturally.

I am an individual like you who has faced a number of challenges in my life. I have had the threat of cancer and the reality of fibroids. Now all that is in my past and today I am happy, healthy, fulfilled, with two beautiful children and I have an abundance of love in my life.

So what made the difference?

Real healing took place when I worked at getting right back to the heart of myself and this book is about getting right to the heart of you. To clearing out the blocks, barriers and debris that you may have accumulated on your life journey. It's the kind of thing most people only do with real commitment when they are facing a serious health challenge.

Having experienced the kind of transformation and healing that can take place when you decide to seriously work on yourself, I wanted to share it. Hence the work I have been doing since 1999 including workshops, talks, teacher training and counselling as well as running several websites.

You have already shown yourself to be someone who is willing to take a leading role in their own healing by reading this book and that is a big part of the process.

You can read my personal story if you want full details further on, but in a nutshell - very many years ago I discovered a lump in my breast and had it surgically removed. A few years later I found another one. I had already begun to realise that cutting bits out of my body was no solution and so I chose not to have surgery. Many years later I discovered I had a large fibroid whilst expecting my first child. A fibroid is a non cancerous tumour or growth. Any doctor will assure you that the only way to eradicate such a growth is by using drugs and/or surgery.

Yet, once I seriously committed to a journey of self healing within months I was sure that the fibroid had shrunk. A year after that original commitment I knew the fibroid and all lumps had gone. This was confirmed for me when I went for a series of scans whilst expecting my second child and they were completely clear.

I know from first hand experience that it is possible to heal your body. I believe that anyone can activate their natural healing process but they have to "get out of their own way" first. By that I mean they have to clear out any barriers or blocks that they hold within to stop this process happening. They also need to create the best environment for the body to heal and that means addressing those unhealthy eating habits, lack of exercise and dedicated "me" time.

In this book I will take you through the process that worked for me, explaining why the various facets are important. I want to provide you with a no-nonsense, no waffle guide.

I am well aware of the fear that takes hold and the pain that can be involved when we face serious health challenges, so be assured I am not sitting in judgement of anyone who opts to have surgery or take the traditional medical route.

I want to empower you to make changes that will transform your world and you can use this after surgery if your health is severely threatened and you haven't got the time to try this first. Only you know what choice is right for you.

I have watched hundreds of people transform right in front of my eyes in a matter of days whilst attending my workshop. Ideally I would like to meet you and work with you through this process. As this is not possible for everyone I have outlined everything you need to know and do in this book. You will follow the same process I did.

Make a firm commitment to yourself to carry it through and actually do the exercises rather than just read them. I know they are sometimes uncomfortable but they are effective.

Whatever you do I know you deserve health and happiness.

How to Use This Book

The best way to use this book is to work your way through each section step by step as it is arranged here. This is a process so skipping a section and moving forward will not serve you and will hinder that process.

Take your time with each section, this is not a race to heal, this is an opening and releasing process. We are working on changing your perspective at a really fundamental level. You will be learning how your emotional and psychological wounds become physical and how to release those wounds from your life. You have held many sub conscious beliefs and patterns of behaviour for most of your life (possibly since the age of 4) so you can allow a few weeks to gently start erasing anything that is causing you pain or "dis-ease" within your body. That is worth taking your time over.

It helps to schedule in some time to do certain exercises. Do not start an exercise if you think you will be disturbed in the middle of it, and always allow extra time following the exercise as a "recovery period". You will be amazed at how tired or slightly tearful you can feel after some of them. These are good signs by the way!

Audio Exercises

Whenever I refer to audio exercises you will find these on your *Release & Heal CD* which is included at the back of the book.

My Healing Experience

Background

Born the youngest child with two brothers, as I look back now over family photographs the one thing that strikes me is how we are never smiling. For me there always seemed to be a feeling of waiting for the next "bad thing" to happen.

As a young child I had lots of headaches, the usual illnesses, plenty of colds and many ear infections and earaches resulting in surgery on one of my ears. I cannot remember a time when we did not have loads of pills and medications in the house.

My Mother had a form of Spina Bifida (malformation of the spine) resulting in her having a colostomy and ileostomy after she had us. She suffered a great deal of pain as well as many infections and the doctors started more serious pain medication and gave her pethidine via injection. Pethidine belongs to a group of medicines called opioid analgesics. It is most commonly used during and after surgery and to relieve pain during childbirth. Pethidine over a long period becomes addictive.

The days were broken up into a few hours before the district nurses would return to our home to give my mother the injection for which she would have been waiting for the past hour. We never knew when the next hospital stay was likely.

In my early years my Father travelled a fair bit with his work which upset my Mother and as time went by I had the impression that he felt helpless in this situation. I always felt that it was my job to "sort things out".

Some years later my Mother was given a spinal block which would stop the pain. At that time it was an experimental procedure which we had tracked down after a television programme featured it. The trouble was that they immediately stopped all medication following the operation. As you can imagine my Mother was a drug addict by this time and so she was climbing the walls and gradually sank into a very dark clinical depression.

Lumps in my Breast

At this time I discovered I had a lump in my breast. I was helping take care of my Mother and renovating a property. I was frightened so kept it to myself for quite a while and started reading "You Can Heal Your Life" by Louise Hay, I also started a macrobiotic diet hoping to kick-start my healing, and took some training in reflexology.

A specialist advised me to have the lump removed and avoid risk as we could not be sure if it was benign or malignant and this seemed like a fairly sensible course of action. The lump was removed and turned out to be benign.

After removal and whilst recovering in my hospital bed the other women on my ward started to tell me that I should expect more lumps as they all had several. I asked the surgeon and he confirmed that I could expect more lumps as most of his patients had several recurrences. However, he could not tell me why I would have them or how to prevent them. I had read somewhere that the contraceptive pill may have something to do with lumps in the breast, neither my Doctor nor specialist could confirm this but I took the decision to stop taking it.

The book had inspired me to make changes but somehow I found it difficult to keep it up, especially after surgery, as the immediate threat had gone. I was back at home involved with my mother who was now mentally unstable and about to go onto a psychiatric ward. It felt like "business as usual".

I am glad to say that my Mother recovered from her depression over a period of months and for the first time in many years was enjoying a more "normal" life.

During all this time I had been in a long term relationship and we had started a business together renovating property. This was really his idea and based on his experience. We had met when we were young and we knew each others backgrounds which helped. He had grown up without the feeling and support of family, I think somewhere inside me I felt that I could fill that hole for him and we could be each others family.

We moved in together to a property we were working on and as usual conditions were uncomfortable with no working bathroom, bare floors and walls. Bit by bit we did up the very large house and it became more comfortable but we were exhausted and under a lot of financial pressure.

About a year later we split up and I felt completely lost. He had found someone else and in one fell swoop I lost the person I loved, my business and home. I felt very ill, could not eat and got very little sleep. I went to the doctor for a weeks worth of sleeping pills because I feared for my sanity.

The practical side of me was well aware that everyone gets their heart broken and that I needed to get a grip. I moved back home temporarily and decided to start again and find interesting work.

My career took off and I was earning good money, getting more of a life of my own. I had my own flat and felt disinclined to spend much time with my parents. I had a few relationships but could not trust, relax and just enjoy them. Underneath I believed that if they got too close and really knew me then they would not want me anymore. I definitely limited my emotional involvement.

A second lump showed up in my breast and although I went to see the specialist and had a mammogram I already knew I would not use surgery again. When I saw the consultant in the hospital he told me that the mammogram showed the lump which looked to be benign but they were unsure and that surgery would give us the answers.

I was amazed when I asked to see the x-ray to find it was missing from my notes (which turned out to be my mothers notes not mine). He told me that although he did not have mine he could show me someone else's and that would be just as good. He then looked at me like I was totally insane when I said that was not acceptable and I wanted to see my own. I never did get to see it.

All of this fed my belief that you could not rely on doctors to come up with a solution, or even care. The decision was a simple one for me, no medical intervention.

After coming home from yet another hospital visit following on from a particularly nasty infection, my mother was behaving differently and seemed to be heading into depression again. She told me that when in hospital someone had given her pethidine for the pain as she was allergic to other pain killers, even though she had asked them not to. Apparently there was nothing marked on her notes to say she should not have it.

She believed, as I do, that it had sparked off a new set of problems from her previous addiction and she was very worried. I had made travel plans months before and a four week trip to America was booked and imminent. I decided to go as so many things had been cancelled in the past because of my mother's illness.

After I left she was taken back into hospital and not long after that she died.

The shock was enormous I was completely stunned and was left feeling if I had not gone to America and had stayed home my Mother would still be alive. A lot of this feeling came from the anecdotal information others gave me on my return about the state of the hospital, dirty conditions and lack of attention my mother received. I felt if I had been there I would have done something about it, after all wasn't that my job?

The interesting thing is that I think my mother knew she would die, when I last saw her and she kissed me goodbye there was something in her eyes. The day she died I had the most enormous headache that just would not shift and if I had not been travelling I would have called home as this quite often happened when she was unwell.

She told me years before, that in her hospital experiences she had seen many women die when it was not expected. They just seemed to make up their minds and that was it. I believe my mother knew that she was headed back into clinical depression, her health was not good and she had spent years fighting and staying active when so many others would have already given up and been bedridden, she was too tired to do it all again.

Her death felt like a huge relief. I felt guilty but also like a weight had lifted.

Discovering my Fibroid

My next main contact with the medical profession was when I became aware of a large fibroid. I was pregnant with my first child in 1995. On my first visit my doctor thought I was expecting twins because of the size of the fibroid and I was immediately seen by a consultant, who diagnosed me with a large pedunculated (on a stalk) fibroid the size of a plate (completely flat) outside the uterine wall.

I was warned that this could put my baby at risk, in the early stages it was growing almost as fast as the baby, fed by the hormones.

This type of fibroid becomes painful because the stalk twists (torsion) and also the fibroid outgrows its blood supply causing it to break down (red degeneration), when this occurs there is also a risk of miscarriage and I was hospitalised for a while when this happened to me.

It is hard to describe the complex mix of emotions I had at the time. I felt very alone, my partner was in America working, I was extremely worried about my baby, who was very much wanted, and seemed at risk because of my condition.

I suppose if I had to sum it up I would say I was lonely and fearful. Health problems in general seem to have a habit of making you feel isolated and alone even when this is not true, but it sort of matched my beliefs that I had better take care of what was going on as no-one else would.

A lot of things blur after the event but one thing I remember very strongly was being in pain and affirming silently and somewhat continuously to my baby that he was staying here with me and I was not going to lose him. I also stopped allowing the doctors to make numerous internal examinations which I felt was putting the baby more at risk than the fibroid.

I count myself as fortunate that I had a natural birth and produced a healthy child who proved to be the gift I knew he was.

After the birth and subsequent follow up months later, the fibroid became the size of a small grapefruit (but flat) and I was told that was the best I could hope for and that it would remain that way until it became a real problem. If and when that happened, I could have it removed after using drugs to shrink it to a more manageable size.

I was also made aware that, just as before with the breast lumps, having had one fibroid, I could have more, and removal would not prevent this. There is such a feeling of hopelessness when someone tells you something like that, but I did not accept it. I knew deep down that my body had created this fibroid and that being the case, it made perfect sense to me that my body could heal itself.

The main challenge was in getting to the root cause so that not only would I get rid of this fibroid but avoid any others.
I am delighted to tell you that I did get to the root cause. I managed to completely dissolve the fibroid myself without any medical intervention.

I achieved this by making some dietary and lifestyle changes but more importantly, by releasing all the negative thoughts, anger, resentment and guilt from my life for past hurts and problems. Intellectually I had an understanding of what was required but never realised just how fundamental to the healing process the releasing and clearing part was.

Let's get started Healing You

Right now I am asking you to open up your mind for this process. You do not have to believe or agree with everything I say just be open to considering it.

Gain a new perspective

As surgery or drugs do not get to the bottom of why you are experiencing this health problem, stop for a moment and consider that your body created this condition and so it is not so very "off the wall" to suggest that your body can also dissolve the condition or heal itself.

The body can usually only communicate distress or dis-ease to you via pain or physical signs, therefore to ignore them or just get rid of the symptoms puts the body under more pressure to get your attention to the real problem.

Surgery has its place and is very valuable especially when a condition is extremely far advanced and time is short to clear it safely. But if this is not the case, whilst still seeing your medical professionals, look within for the answers to your health problem. Surgery and drugs all have side effects, even a stay in hospital can mean catching infection. Always check statistics on "surgical outcomes" for your particular health issue as some surgery only provides a temporary relief.

Please understand that I respect medical practitioners, they speak their truth as I speak mine. They rarely if ever see patients who have healed naturally. By the very nature of their job they see sick people and traditionally use drugs and surgery as the tools of their trade.

Metaphysically what does your illness represent?

If we start by looking at my own health, fibroids usually strike at the very heart of a woman's' femininity and their location gives a clue as to their origins. The probable causes for fibroid cysts and tumours metaphysically are "Nursing a hurt from a partner - a blow to the feminine ego". (Louise L.Hay)

The womb, Uterus and pelvic area are where the process of creation occurs. Whilst a baby can be created, grow and be nurtured in this area it is also seen as the centre for our artistic creativity. When this creativity is stifled in some way then it is in this area that problems will occur.

When I discovered this it made perfect sense as it was certainly true for me on both counts (femininity and creativity). As money had been tight I had been working alongside my partner like a builder on the buildings we renovated and had almost become "one of the lads".

When my partner met a carefree young girl whose only concern was what to wear to Saturday's party. I felt he was understandably drawn to that fresh (and what seemed to me like more feminine) experience. I also felt that he should have appreciated how I had given up so much in trying to make ends meet for the both of us. After all we had been through I felt betrayed. It struck at the very heart of my femininity as I took a good hard look at myself and compared myself to this girl.

However, the button that had been pushed when this happened came from an earlier time not from this event. The really annoying part was that I had never really wanted to work on a building site renovating property. That is not to say that I did not enjoy it sometimes but originally I had wanted to be a fashion designer. All that creativity was given up in favour of what seemed a more practical business like approach that fitted with my family who were very much involved in a masculine business world. In many ways I had been brought up like my brothers and not like a girl at all. So many "girly" things I had wanted to do were given up in favour of more "sensible" pursuits or what fitted with my parent's circumstances and lifestyle.

A lot of anger, guilt, hurt, blame and resentment came up but did not get dealt with appropriately and so ended up pushed down and stored away inside. As a result my body had to deal with it and finally got my attention with the fibroid.

I now realise that any time you deny facets of yourself, give away your personal power, get stuck in the past, start blaming someone else or expecting them to make everything right - then you are setting yourself on a path of unhappiness and ultimately ill health. You start to disconnect from who you really are.

Where are you experiencing health problems?

Just as the location of my fibroid gave me clues as to the nature of my problem and thus how to cure it, your body provides valuable information for you. Later on we will be working with the mind/body link.

The following is a general and by no means exhaustive list of some of the factors that may have contributed to poor health in you:

Relationship Trauma

This could be an extremely painful break-up, disappointment or betrayal in a relationship. Whilst we all experience pain in the break up of a relationship some of us seem to get stuck in that experience. Quite often it was an unhealthy or co-dependent relationship; there may have been lies and deceit. The individual finds themselves running over the entire relationship looking for clues they missed or imagined deceits. Prior negative beliefs and thought processes like not feeling lovable or good enough are involved, usually from childhood. This feeling of disappointment or betrayal can also be associated with others not just a romantic relationship. Sometimes the individual stays stuck in the pain, not having resolved what occurred.

Termination or miscarriage.

Whether male or female, when we interfere with or something goes wrong with this natural biological process we can suffer guilt and feelings of being punished or needing to be, depending on your fundamental and religious beliefs.

I have found with the women I have encountered that whatever the reasons for a termination or how each person rationalises the decision, subconsciously a self critical judgement seems to take place. When it does it is far harsher than any that may be encountered from others.

Sexual abuse in formative years.

This can take many forms and when it begins does not always register as such a terrible thing with a child. The difficulties arise as secrets are kept and as they learn in confusing ways that something is not right about what is going on. This can result in confusion and a feeling that they are "bad" and that their bodies are dirty or that sex is wicked. If there is no-one for them to turn to who can put this right for them or clear up what they may see as their part in it then the guilt, hurt and damage continue.

I have seen a woman who was told by her father intimate details of his sexual needs. Her mother told her about her fathers' inadequacies and her dislike of sex. Neither parent knew the other was talking to her this way. The anger and frustration that built up for her in this environment of secrecy was almost unbearable and robbed her of her childhood. She could not share this with anyone and felt isolated. Understandably this caused problems in her intimate relationships in adulthood.

I have seen several individuals who have experienced incest. Although confused and unsure, some were initially grateful for the attention and apparent love (which seemed to be missing generally in the family). They started to become isolated as they had to keep secrets and realised that they were doing something wrong. In some cases they also suffered rejection as the abuse stopped, sometimes (in the case of girls) when periods started. Thus linking rejection to their sexual development or bodily functions.
Whilst both boys and girls suffer, boys in particular have no one to share their feelings with and so everything gets trapped inside. This is also especially true for those who knew what was going on was "wrong" and hated it but felt no one would believe them or that the adults around them seemed to condone it.

Whatever takes place colours their future relationship beliefs and experiences.

Difficult Childhoods

Some have been let down in their childhood, unable to rely on their parents, maybe having had to take control and become the adult too young. I have come across many who had to practically "bring up" siblings because their parents were incapacitated through alcoholism, drugs, poor health or depression. Some were from single parent families and suffered a succession of dysfunctional "step" fathers/mothers. This brings up safety issues. Feeling let down or unsupported can take many forms even down to never knowing if your parents would be home when you got in from school, or feeling that you could not talk through concerns. As adults, again we rationalise what happened but that does not release it from our systems. Also as adults as we learn from others that we could have had a better childhood, this brings a sense of loss that may not have been felt at the time.

I had found myself at a young age consulting with doctors
and trying to keep things in the family home on an even keel.
What I was seeing was one adult who was getting more ill
and becoming an addict and the other one opting out of
dealing with what was happening. So many fun trips or
promised times were cancelled that I stopped expecting good
things to happen.
I have seen may men who as a child felt they had to become
the "man of the house" when their father left and their
mother seemed unable to cope.

Taking Care of Others

Taking care of other peoples needs too much, a feeling of having to
earn love, kindness, attention etc. I have come across numerous men
and women who felt unwanted as a child, often being told so. Quite
often they are from large Catholic families where their mothers
struggled to cope. Others were told that their parents wanted a boy
(or a girl), or that they considered abortion. They were continually
trying to make up for something that was not their fault. Again if
there were a succession of new partners coming into the home then
there was a feeling of having to please others to ensure attention and
survival.

One woman's mother attempted to strangle her when she
said she was not going to continue with college, her brother
saved her. Her mother had given up on her own dreams at a
very young age with a marriage and lots of children and she
had put her hopes on her daughter fulfilling them. She had
always been particularly hard on her daughter and held a
lot of anger.

I know my Mother had a hard time when she was pregnant
with me and that my birth may have been the final straw that
brought about all her surgeries. I had been taken away from
her immediately after my birth to be looked after
temporarily by an aunt. Whilst my aunt was a wonderful
woman she seemed to have no idea what to do with babies. I

23

always felt that if I was useful enough, helpful enough and was needed then people may just love me. So I worked at keeping others happy and worried about their needs far more than my own. Metaphysically speaking the lumps I developed in my breast indicated that I was "over mothering".

Giving Up on Dreams

Giving up on dreams (usually for practical reasons or to fulfil someone else's needs), not using natural gifts or talents, stifled creativity. Many people get to their 30's or 40's and feel unfulfilled but are not sure why. If you have this feeling it may be that you stopped following your hearts desire and passion. Perhaps you took on a particular job or role to be "sensible" or because "needs must". Those who have spent their childhood taking care of their parent or siblings (acting as a mother/father), or who had children very young, will have put so much of their lives on hold they may be totally unaware of what their dreams are or ever were.

Strict Religious Upbringing

I have met and spoken with many who were brought up in the Catholic faith and occasionally in a strict Anglican Church family. They always felt guilty with regards to sex and their bodies as they have been taught of temptation and wickedness that can come from such things. As young people grow and discover their bodies, if they come across messages that tell them even thinking about their bodies in a sexual way is evil, then they start to believe something must be wrong with them or they are "bad". What was originally designed to assist young people to remain safe and living in the "right" way, turns into something twisted and stops them being able to discuss their concerns. Further they may believe they are "damned". Your parents, like mine, may have felt very uncomfortable with anything to do with sex and it was never discussed in our family. This can just leave an uncomfortable feeling that something is not right.

Shallow Breathing

We tend to tense parts of our body as a response to physical and emotional stress. Women more than men seem to breathe from their upper chest rather than a full round breath filling the lower lungs. Some women subconsciously tense the pelvic muscles, which blocks the blood flow and cuts off the supply of nutrients to their organs. This area is where I held most of my "stuff" but was totally unaware of it. Over a long period of time this area becomes shut off and desensitised. When the oxygen levels drop in the muscles, lactic acid is produced which causes cramping & discomfort. Muscles need a good blood flow in order to help toxins be removed.

> *See if this is true for you. Notice if you are tensing any parts of your body especially your abdomen. Right now as you read this just take in a series of deep breaths and let them out slowly and just notice how different your body feels.*

Grief

The death of a close friend, loved one (including pets) or family member most often brings strong feelings of sadness and loneliness. Fear and anxiety are also common. Some people also experience feelings of resentment, anger, and guilt. Whilst experiencing any or all of these emotions following a loss is perfectly normal, when these feelings are very strong and persistent, possibly accompanied by certain types of disturbing thoughts, the natural healing and recovery process of grief is delayed or even halted. Another way of saying this is that the bereaved person becomes "stuck". When this happens the bereaved person, in a sense, loses their own life. This can lead to depression and many other health problems.

Did you identify with any of the above?

You may or may not have identified with any of the above contributing factors; if not just notice if when you read any of them they annoyed you or made you feel uncomfortable. That discomfort may be an indicator of an area that needs some attention.

This is not about blaming you, your parents, relatives, lovers or friends. We do not need to point the finger anywhere. We just need to be aware of certain factors in our lives that may have contributed to our condition so that we can release or clear anything that is holding us back from healing.

What has become clear to me over the years and I hope is becoming clear to you, is how our emotional and psychological wounds become physical. I believe the releasing of all that "old stuff" was absolutely essential to my own physical healing. I am not alone in that belief.

Here is an example from the book "Women's Bodies, Women's Wisdom" written by Dr. Christiane Northrup:

"I found a small fibroid in Gina, a patient who was thirty eight years old at the time. I asked her to meditate on "blocked energy" in her pelvis, and she later told me, "when I got home and took some time with this question, I realised that when my brother died in an accident, I was furious with him for leaving. I was twenty five and really couldn't allow myself to feel that rage. So I just stuffed it in my pelvis. I hadn't thought about that for years". On a follow up examination three months later, I found that her fibroid was gone. I believe that by expressing and experiencing the full impact of her anger for the first time, she changed the energy pattern in her pelvis and actually dematerialised the fibroid, transforming it from matter into energy".

She also adds *"I've seen other women decrease or eliminate their fibroids when they remembered and released old experiences".*

You will find many anecdotal and documented examples for yourself for just about every ailment you can imagine or have experienced. The key point here is not the condition given in that example but the understanding that your body can heal itself when you release whatever it is that you are holding onto. So, the important thing now is to get started on your own releasing and *healing from the inside out.*

Making a Commitment to Yourself

From here on in I will share with you techniques for releasing and bringing about the changes you need. Try not to think in terms of curing yourself of whatever health challenge you are facing. Think of yourself as a whole person realising your full potential. You are far more than the symptoms you are presenting, and the dis-ease just represents those disowned parts of yourself, hurts, anger and other emotions. But they are from your past and all we want to do now is clear them out of your body to be replaced by health and happiness.

With this book you have access to guided meditations and exercises and it is important that you take full advantage of these. Most people find they have resistance to doing any kind of change related personal work so let's take a look at that.

First let's get some of those immediate barriers out of the way. Some of these may include:

- these "self help" programmes don't work;

- past disappointments or "failed" attempts at making changes;

- the thought that it has to be a painful experience;

- the fear of the unknown "better the devil you know than the devil you don't";

- thoughts like "the kind of stuff I've got will take years to clear" or "I'll probably have to do weird hippy type stuff".

All of these are just thoughts and thoughts can be changed. That was yesterday, this is today.

I do not require you to fully believe in this programme I just want you to do what I ask you to as you work your way through.

Let me reassure you, change does not have to be painful. It can often just be a release from the past, opening you up again to the joy and wonder of life and its infinite possibilities, in much the same way as children see life.

When you decide to visit a friend in the car, you may check directions and then you get in your car and set off knowing where it is you want to get to. The journey may take you a while and into unfamiliar territory, but you don't keep stopping or pop back home in between. You never doubt that you will arrive. You do not spend the whole journey questioning yourself about it. You just do it!

It is the same with this process, it is a journey within. From time to time it may feel slightly uncomfortable but it is a forward motion and if you just keep going you will get to your destination – being healthy, healed and whole.

As human beings we have a variety of "avoidance" methods, ways in which we opt out of doing something we do not want to do or fear doing. One of yours may be in becoming so busy you do not have time to do this, or putting it off because you feel unwell.

The techniques we use here are cathartic and cleansing. They may not be what you are used to but they are mostly based on Cognitive behavioural techniques and similar tried and tested methods. Change can happen very quickly once you are truly ready. It is almost like turning on a light or a page in a book but you still need to take the steps required.

Sometimes events can cause this change instantaneously as for example those who have a "near death experience" or have experienced a life threatening event or illness. Often referred to as a "wake up call" suddenly your priorities change. Petty hurts and grudges, worrying about small day to day practicalities and what has gone on in the past, are wiped away by the clarity that comes from the realisation it was all so nearly over. There really is more to life, and in particular your life, than that.

Many say that their life only really began after they were diagnosed with cancer. After dropping all their personal baggage, illusions and pretence to reclaim themselves. This is a time that true healing can take place as we strip away the layers of conditioning we experienced and the masks we use. Then we can find out what and who we really are right down in our very soul.

But rather than thinking in terms of something horrible that needs to be done, some process that has to be gone through, I want you to look on this as an exciting opportunity. One that you will look back on as the turning point that allowed you to bring the joy back into your life.

People who attend my workshops and sessions come for lots of different reasons, all have one thing in common they have reached a point in their lives where they have taken a firm decision to change things. On some level things are not working well. They know that continuing on in the same old way and feeling out of control is never going to bring the things they want into their lives. They take back responsibility for moving on and this act alone starts the process of change and can bring about the necessary healing.

As far as working on yourself and your healing is concerned, don't wait any longer, decide to make those changes now.

Set your intention:

"I now commit to healing, nurturing and loving myself".

Keep working with this intention for the rest of today at least. Write it on some "post it" notes and stick them around the house to remind you.

The following are techniques for getting the process underway. I discuss the pros and cons of attending workshops or sessions with a practitioner a little later.

Books are wonderful fountains of knowledge and reading is a beneficial and enjoyable pastime but in the quest to live the life you have dreamed of, you have to get on with the practical stuff as well or it all remains an intellectual exercise.

This book is not holiday reading, use this book almost like a text book, do the exercises, do not put them off. Feel the shift taking place in your consciousness.

Be your biggest supporter - you are embarking on a voyage of discovery within and about yourself. It all begins and ends with you so give yourself all the support you need on this adventure. Now go and buy yourself a great looking new A5 or A4 notebook and find a good pen that you will enjoy writing with. Make them something special that you will enjoy using. Yes, it is worth making the effort to get something nice for yourself, we want to make this an adventure that you will enjoy.

SUMMARY

Be open to the possibility that your body can heal itself.

Make a firm commitment to yourself to do this process properly.

Set your intention: "I now commit to healing, nurturing and loving myself".

Find a notebook and pen you will enjoy using ready for the exercises that will follow.

Awareness Raising

Exercise 1 - Let's do a Stock-take

 This will only take you about two minutes so do not read on just get a pen and paper. When you are ready, work through the list below rating on a scale of 1 to 10 (with 1 being bad to 10 being great) how each area of your life is doing right now. e.g. health – if I am experiencing perfect health I would put 10, if I had challenges and seemed to be constantly unwell I might put 3. Trust your own judgement this is for your use only. Be honest with yourself.

Health (physical)

Health (emotional)

Sense of Purpose

Career

Primary Relationship (partner/spouse, lover)

Relationships (family, friends)

Work relationships (colleagues, boss)

Support from friends

Sense of well-being

Assertiveness

Spirituality

Wealth/prosperity

Take a look at the numbers you have put in that last exercise, they can show you where imbalances in your life are. No judgements here just raising awareness.

Have you got your notebook and pen yet? If you have, then continue on with the next exercise.

Exercise 2 – Opening Up Process

This is an audio exercise available on your *Release & Heal CD*. Listen to track 1 - the introduction, then track 2 - the chant and meditation, followed by track 3 - the guidance. This is an opening up process.

Once you have done this audio exercise (please do not skip it, it really is important). Take a break for at least a day before you continue on and do exercise 3 part 1.

Exercise 3 - Review to date looking for patterns.

Exercise 1 gave you a snapshot of where you are at the moment.

Exercise 2 started getting you in touch with your sub-conscious.

Now I would like you to look into the past and see what brought you here.

This exercise requires time and a fair bit of writing. This is unlike the other exercises you will encounter and probably the most time consuming. After this one we will be working more with the sub-conscious again and meditation. So don't let this put you off continuing.

Allow a full morning or afternoon to start Part 1 when you will be undisturbed by people, calls, work etc. Get out your new notebook and pen. Disconnect the telephone and make it clear that you are unavailable. This does require discipline but is key to the process so give it your best shot.

Part 1

Write about your life to date in ten year chunks e.g. The first ten years. The first ten are often the most crucial (but not for everyone) so start there and then take a break and review what you have written.

If you are finding it difficult to focus your attention use a series of questions to assist you such as:

what is your earliest memory? ;
Who was your first best friend? ;
What school did you go to? ;
Who in your life had the most impact on you (or who do you remember best)?

You may be finding it difficult to settle to this task, if that is the case then you are experiencing the very natural phenomena of resistance. You may be trying to avoid doing it by suddenly becoming aware of so many other things you have to do. If you knuckle down and get on with it, this will pass.

Tell yourself you will work hard on this for thirty minutes or an hour and then take a break. Breaking it down in this way stops it seeming to stretch out before you as an endless task.

When you are able to, continue with the next ten years and so on until you hit whatever period is crucial to you. It is worth continuing anyway as you may start to see patterns developing.

Finish each ten year block by summarising the events and people who had the most lasting impact on you and why.
When you have completed this just review what you have written. This is your life story and it is a rare chance to just look at your life and see what has been going on and where your beliefs and patterns may have come from. No need to judge yourself in any way just think of it as research.

Check in With Yourself

Throughout this process it is important to regularly take heed of how you are feeling (reacting).

Take note of how you are feeling right now and how you have felt after each exercise. You may have a headache, feel slightly unwell or like you are going down with a cold. These are signs that there is something challenging going on inside and this is a bit like a detox. We are challenging your core beliefs. What you believe to be true becomes true for you so again I want to remind you to think of  yourself as healthy, healed and whole. I also want you to drink lots of water to assist the body to flush out whatever is being released.

Well done for getting this far. It really does get easier.

You have done enough for now so just decide when you can next set aside an hour or more for Part 2 and schedule it in.

Part 2 – Review Continued

Take each of the headings from the stock take (exercise 1) in turn and think through everything to do with it.

As an example - for relationships:

Try to recall your mother and fathers' or carers relationship

Were they openly loving?

Did you feel loved?

How was love expressed in your family?

How was anger expressed?

Did you feel safe?

Now widen the scope to close friends and lovers. Have you had healthy happy relationships? Most people get their heart broken but generally has there been any violence or bad behaviour involved on yours or the other persons' part?

Start looking for patterns of behaviour that may have been repeated or similar to those experienced in childhood e.g. do your partners always cheat on you, are they violent, are you the underdog? Likewise note down the positive trends.

Then work through each of the other topics, write down the headings and make brief notes (write more if you like). Do not be too quick to cover a heading, again that can be avoidance. If once you have moved on, a memory comes back to you, just jot it down under the appropriate heading before you forget.

Whilst this can seem like a bit of a chore to start with you would be amazed at how much starts to come back to you once you get into it.

If you find yourself getting tearful or feeling upset, uncomfortable or angry whilst writing, then take note of what you were thinking or writing when those feelings started to arise and make a note of it. Allow the tears and emotion to flow, this is a process of getting back in touch with your inner self and releasing old hurt, anger and negativity which may have been locked in for too long. Let it go!

Any emotions or feelings, even resistance, are signs that you are starting to get in touch with facets of yourself and areas that need attention. Allow yourself the joy of that confirmation and know that this is one of the most fascinating and rewarding journeys of your life.

Do not read on unless you have done the previous exercises, take action now.

The only thing stopping you from having a life you love is you.

SUMMARY

Do a quick stock take by completing exercise 1.

When you have 30 minutes to spare listen to the first audio introduction and exercise on your *Release & Heal CD*.

Review your life in 10 year blocks looking for patterns

Check in with yourself, do a quick body scan and check how you feel.

Review the stock take topics in more depth.

Loving Yourself – Extreme Self Care

Even as you read the title for this section I wonder if you felt any resistance. The concept of loving yourself can be difficult for people to get to grips with for several different reasons such as:

Many people associate "loving yourself" with ego and selfishness especially in relationships. You may have heard someone say "he loves himself!" in a negative fashion when a confident, attractive man enters the room.

Religion teaches us quite often that we must put others first, that we need to work hard to earn forgiveness for our sins and so forth.

As we grow up our parents or Carers may have given us the impression that we had to earn their love by being good, getting good results or behaving in certain ways. We may have felt that we always disappointed them.

We may have been abused or mistreated at some stage in our lives, leading us to believe that we were so ugly, stupid, wicked or guilty, that we do not deserve or can never attract love.

We may believe because of something we did at some time e.g. abortion, that we are evil or "bad" even "damned" and hate parts of ourselves or our personality.

We all experience what we call a "broken heart" at some point in our lives either from a failed love affair or the death of someone (animal or person) that we love. It then seems like a huge risk to love again. Some of us believe that love is too risky and painful and cannot be trusted, so we shut off the loving parts of ourselves.

All of the above and many more reasons exist for individuals not to love themselves and I come across them all the time. These are my thoughts on that:

As far as ego and selfishness go I like to use the analogy of being on an aeroplane.

Whenever you fly anywhere the stewardess goes through an explanation of what to do in the event of a crash or emergency. The instructions she gives the passengers makes it clear that in such an event you put your own life jacket and oxygen mask on first and then onto any accompanying children or elderly relatives.

Why?

You cannot help anyone if you are drowning, unable to breathe or dead. The likelihood is you will get in the way and prevent others from escaping.

In the same way, you cannot love another and they will find it extremely hard to love you, unless you love yourself.

No matter what your religion you will find the same advice of loving yourself in amongst the texts and prayers that you hear. For example – the commandment to "love thy neighbour as thy self", it does not say as you would love a friend or relative it says "as yourself". So you have to start from that base first, accepting that it was always what was intended

As far as parental influence is concerned there may be a whole host of negative thoughts and emotions running through you that make you believe you are unlovable from simple statements like "you are lazy/ bad/ trouble" to worse, as in "I never wanted you". These things may not have been said but implied, they may not even have been true, but the net result is the same.

As a parent myself I also understand that even when you love your children completely and unconditionally you still have to keep them safe and teach them basic right and wrong. These many teaching messages can be misinterpreted such as "if you are good you will have a treat" can translate into only "good children" or those who have earned nice things get treats. The love, treat or whatever is directly linked to how lovable they are.

The reasons for your resistance to loving yourself can be ascertained, acknowledged and released as you progress with the various exercises. I strongly urge you not to get bogged down in that but to go straight for loving yourself now.

Dr. Darren Weissman in his book "The Power of Infinite Love and Gratitude" says:

"To be healed means to become whole...Becoming whole means bringing all of ourselves into the light, leaving nothing in the dark, no matter how disturbing or painful it may be. It is an embracing of all the parts we have ignored, denied, tried to push away or eliminate. Healing brings all of this into the conscious mind, into our hearts, into our lives".

Right now in these early stages of the process I would like you to treat yourself with extreme self care. I would love to hear you jumping up and down and shouting "me, me, me ..." I am certain that on many levels your needs have often been put on the back burner, now is the time to make yourself your priority.

How do I do it?

Essentially the first and most important key to your healing is the belief that you are a loving and amazing human being. Someone who deserves all good in their life including perfect health, no matter what has happened in the past. As you are experiencing dis-ease or discomfort, on some level you are not accepting this and certainly not loving yourself. Someone, something or several events lead you to the belief that you are not lovable. It is only you who can change that belief.

Accept now that loving yourself has nothing to do with ego, feeling you are better than anyone else or selfishness. It is all about accepting yourself exactly as you are today "warts and all".

Start appreciating the opportunity for life that you have been given, for taking care of the miracle that you are, for understanding that everyone has a right to thrive and flourish and reach their full potential and everyone is worth loving.

Most of us spend a good deal of our time and energy chasing after love and seeking approval from others. We feel if we look right, make ourselves useful, fit in with others plans or views of what is right then we can make others love us.

The truth is there is only one person you can depend on to be there and to stay with you from birth until death and that is you.

Because everyone always seems to want to know how to love themselves in a nutshell upfront there now follows the *"Gillian Bowles Quick Guide to loving Yourself"* which will then be followed by more in depth guidance.

My Quick Guide on How to Start Loving Yourself

Start putting yourself first. Know that in working on and healing yourself you will make life more wonderful not just for you but for everyone around you. Adopt the belief that you are a truly amazing individual, loving and lovable (even if you do not believe it at the outset). Think about all that you have achieved in your life. Just getting this far is an achievement. You have probably rarely given thought to just how much you have done, learned, overcome or coped with. Celebrate your successes and think about all that you are yet to achieve as a healthy, happy, beautiful individual.

Use meditation daily if only for 10 – 15 minutes. Regularly visualise yourself as a happy, healthy, whole person surrounded by love, in what ever scenario feels fantastic to you.

Notice if you are critical of others or yourself and stop. Usually if you find yourself criticising others then inside and sub consciously you are criticising yourself even more harshly. Likewise if you find yourself being criticised by others, there is something going on inside you. Stop all criticism. Criticism never changes a thing. Refuse to criticize yourself. Accept yourself exactly as you are. Everyone makes mistakes. Everybody changes. When you criticize yourself, your changes are negative. When you approve of yourself, your changes are positive.

Stop holding yourself responsible for others. Their lives are their business. When you love yourself you do not hurt yourself, nor do you hurt or interfere in someone else's life. Respect other peoples choices and decisions. It is not your role to "save" someone from themselves. Empower them to find their own solutions to whatever life brings. Lead by example. Be a healthy, happy, loving presence in their lives.

Praise yourself. Just as Criticism breaks the inner spirit, praise builds it up. Praise yourself as much as you can. Tell yourself how well you are doing with every little thing. We are all good at something. Then start extending this to others.

Use positive affirmations (thoughts and words) especially when challenges arise. Do not terrorize yourself with your thoughts. If you find yourself spiralling down into negativity "stop the rot" find a mental image that gives you pleasure, (my children's smiles work for me) and immediately switch your scary thought to a calming positive thought.

Use the mirror to empower your affirmations. Look into your own eyes often in the mirror and use positive affirmations. Express this growing sense of love you have for yourself. Forgive yourself if you feel you have done something less than you wanted to. At least once a day look into the mirror and say: "I love you".

Release yourself and others from the past. Stop holding onto old grudges and events. No matter how justified, being trapped in self righteousness brings bitterness and sucks the joy out of life. Let it go. Yes, you can get to a place of forgiveness.

Take care of your body. Learn about nutrition. What kind of food does your body need for optimum health? You will find some basic guidelines in this book and you can start to introduce some of those immediately. What kind of exercise can you enjoy? There is something for everyone – swimming, aerobics, pilates, yoga, boxercise, Tai Chi etc. Walking is an excellent way to start, just twenty minutes medium paced walking at least three times a week gets the circulation going and the muscles toning. The body is the house you live in so get it in order.

Understand that you are learning a new way of being. Be gentle with yourself. Be kind to yourself. Be patient with yourself as you learn these new ways of thinking and being.

Find ways to support yourself. Reach out to friends and allow them to help you. It is being strong to ask for help when you need it. Go for a massage or reflexology. Take time out for yourself and do what refreshes and nurtures you.

Acknowledge your dark side. Oh yes we all have one or more. If you try and lock them away in a cupboard they will jump out and take control when you least expect it. It is normal not to be perfect. Any what you might call "negative personality traits" you have, just acknowledge that you created them to fulfil a need. Now you are finding new, positive ways to fulfil those needs. So, lovingly release the old negative patterns.

The most wonderful and comfortable people to be around are those who are comfortable with and love and accept themselves as they are. They have no hidden agendas; they do not need to manipulate to get love as they already have a firm foundation.

An extra bonus - confident, happy loving people are very attractive, so let's get on with it.

We have already covered why loving yourself is so important so now we are going to develop the other themes.

Practising Meditation

Meditation is a very useful tool for just general relaxation right up to more serious personal work and I now want you to add in the habit of a short meditation each day.

Initially learning to sit quietly with your eyes closed for 10-15 minutes on a regular basis will train your body to relax when you want it to.

At the beginning the mind is very busy and there is a lot of chatter going on. Gradually you will notice that your mind and body quieten down. This provides a wonderful opportunity to get in touch with your own inner wisdom.

How many times have you said (or thought) "I just need some peace or time to think?" especially when you are seeking a solution to a problem or have an important decision to make. That is because you instinctively know that you have all the answers inside even if you cannot access them.

Scientists have tested people whilst meditating and have seen the brainwave patterns change before their eyes (on their machine readouts) blood pressure drops and breathing slows. So even if you are not into the Zen Buddhist approach and remove all spiritual reference, you can understand the benefits that meditating can bring.

I believe so strongly in the importance of meditating for mental, physical and emotional health that I produced two specific guided meditation CDs purely for this particular kind of healing work – the **Heal Your Life CD** and **Heartfelt Affirmations CD** (S*ee resources section)*

What can you expect to experience?

Initially you are likely to just experience some relaxation. When you listen to a guided meditation like the ones on the accompanying *Release & Heal CD*, then you may experience emotions which can include anger and sadness. This is a good thing as it means you are releasing these feelings which may have been held inside you for a long time.

As you practise meditation more, you will find these brief moments of calm as restoring, healing and ultimately essential to a happy healthy life. In these busy times we rarely get the opportunity to get back in touch with ourselves. As time goes by they will bring you joy and a sense of bliss.

We all have an inner child just wanting us to listen for once and do the things that bring us joy, we also have a wise and "higher self" who will answer all our questions if we listen.

Unless we take quiet time and put ourselves into an appropriate state to receive this information, it doesn't get through. These facets of ourselves will then try and get our attention another way via illness, discomfort or sudden emotional outbursts which surprise us and seemingly come from no-where.

Give it a go, you have absolutely nothing to lose and health and happiness to gain!

How to take time out to Meditate Daily

There are many ways of meditating, everyone can do it and there is no right or wrong way. The important thing to begin with is just taking quiet time for yourself.

46

Make sure you will not be disturbed in order to relax fully, so take the telephone off the hook (for the sake of ten to fifteen minutes people can wait) - change your answer-phone message if you like.

You can start with just 10 minutes and progress to longer periods if you wish, however, meditating for an hour or two will not necessarily make the experience more worthwhile. Regular short meditations are far more valuable in my experience than an hour long burst every now and again, but you will work out what feels right for you.

Lie down or sit comfortably in a well supported chair.

I find that laying down suits me best if I have about 30 minutes to spare. My body is totally supported, my spine is straight, my arms are alongside my body palms uppermost and my body automatically knows that it is supposed to relax.

If I only have 10 - 15 minutes then I tend to sit in a chair, again I make sure that my back is supported and that my feet touch the ground and are flat on the floor (ladies it helps to remove your shoes!). Try both ways and see which one feels right for you.

Allow your mind to quieten its' thoughts, and the body to completely relax.

There are many ways to quieten your mind and body here are a few:

- Focusing on your breath - slowing the pace of your breathing, noticing the coolness of the breath entering your nostrils.

- If you practise yoga you could do some alternate nostril breathing.

- It is important to breathe in through the nose if possible as the body tends to breathe rapidly through the mouth when highly active or in fight or flight.

- Counting down from ten to one slowly

- Visualising yourself walking down a very long staircase, getting more relaxed as you go further down

- in a similar vein you could visualise yourself as a leaf falling from a tree in Autumn and gently floating down to the earth knowing that you go deeper and become more relaxed the closer you get to the earth.

- once you have done some visualisation you can create your own inner sanctuary, a place where you feel safe and relaxed and the more you use that visualisation the easier and quicker it becomes to achieve relaxation under any circumstance.

- Music can be very helpful in "putting you in the mood", however, it needs to be very much in the background and non-intrusive. If you start to get involved in listening to the music you may just take a walk down memory lane and what we actually want here is to slow thought right down and go within.

- Affirmations can be useful initially when you settle down just as you breathe in and out say "I am.....relaxed" or something similar. We will look more at affirmations a little later.

Once calm and quiet just stay in that state for a while or introduce a question such as "What is it I need to know?" This does not presuppose the answer and allows any topic that needs your attention to come up. Do not try to consciously answer the question yourself, just remain quiet and go with the flow. If something has been bothering you then the chances are following meditation that the solution will come to you, seemingly out of the blue.

To come out of meditation, when you are ready reverse your relaxation process by counting up from 1 to 10 or visualising climbing back up the stairs etc. If time is an issue for you on any occasion do not use an alarm of any sort to bring you out of meditation. Either use a guided meditation recording (on the Heal Your Life CD use any of the last three tracks that follow a chant with five minutes quiet music) or play a piece of music you know that lasts 10-15 minutes, so that you will gently know when to come out of it.

Finish your meditation by affirming that – "today is a wonderful day, what I need to know is revealed to me and what I need comes to me, all is well in my world".

Practise meditating as often as you can and find the way that works best for you.

So now that you have read through the basic instructions time to give it a try. From now on I want you to do 15 minutes every day of just sitting and quieting the mind. If you use a regular time each day it will make it easier and become a good habit. First thing in the morning can be a good time and sets you up for the day.

SUMMARY

Put yourself first and start practising "extreme self-care".

Practise meditating daily, experimenting with different techniques until you find the one that suits you best. Setting a regular time really helps, it just takes 15 minutes.

Do not move on if you have not started meditation practise.

Using the Mind/Body link for Healing

Using the Mind/Body link for healing is not a new technique. Ancient healing practices, for example traditional Chinese medicine and Ayurvedic medicine, emphasise the importance of the mind/body link in healing. Hippocrates wrote, "The natural healing force within 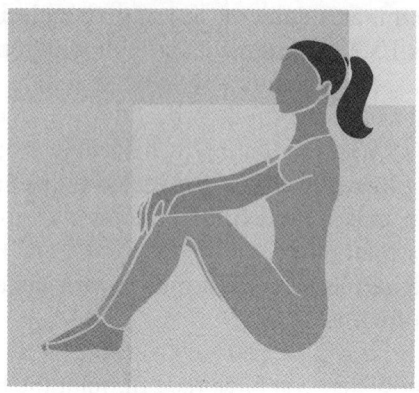 each one of us is the greatest force in getting well".

In Western society, whilst phrases such as "mind over matter" have been around for years, it is only fairly recently scientists have found solid evidence that mind/body techniques actually do combat disease and promote health.

Mind/body techniques are helpful for many conditions. At the very least they promote relaxation, improve coping skills, reduce tension and pain, and lessen the need for medication.

Whilst it can still be quite a leap of faith and thinking to accept that your thoughts and past experiences have created whatever health or other challenge you are currently facing, we often have first hand evidence. As women we soon become aware of how emotional upsets or extra stress affect our menstrual cycle. Most of us have heard of the "placebo effect", where a sugar pill is given to a patient and yet the patients' body still reacts and gets better as if they received the normally prescribed effective medication.

We live in exciting times when science and medicine are proving the case for certain alternative approaches.

Stress, that much over used term, is another good example of the Mind/Body link. Stress hormones are associated with particular emotions like anger and resentment. These hormones affect systems and organs throughout the body. But stress is not always bad. Some stress is inevitable and actually beneficial. If you think in terms of building muscles, unless you put your muscles under stress they do not develop greater strength and tone. Stress can assist people attain goals and perform their best.

Everyone's tolerance for stress is different, and each person handles it differently depending on their background and belief system. It is important to recognize your limits and this is easy if you are in touch with and listen to your body's messages.

Your body will give you warning signs which will tell you when your stressors (i.e. work load, relationships, health etc.) are too much for you to handle safely. For some it may start with a headache or a stomach ache, tension in the neck, shoulders or back, exhaustion, insomnia, digestive problems, irritability or agitation. Over a prolonged period of time this will lead to poor health and depression.

What Gives Stress its Power?

What gives stress its power in your life is you and your thoughts.

If you feel trapped, out of control or in a "no win situation" your stress levels will rise and things will become intolerable. Such a situation can occur if you are someone who cares for an elderly infirm parent or other member of the family. This is particularly so if you are caring for children and an elderly parent with for example alzheimers. You would naturally feel trapped and unable to see a good way out.

A study by scientists at Ohio State University suggests that the chronic stress of Care-giving affects a critical pathway in the immune system in the long term. This results in chronic health problems like heart disease, arthritis, type 2 diabetes and certain cancers. They also found that their reduced immunity continued long after they ceased to be Carers.

Generally, research shows that being stressed and having negative emotions is unhealthy. Unconsciously being defensive or stifling feelings will result in serious medical consequences, such as high blood pressure. High blood pressure is also associated with feelings of hopelessness. How a person processes emotions also affects how long he or she may survive a chronic illness.

The word "stress" could most often be replaced by the word "Fear".

Think about it we get stressed as we fear the worst. Exam stress is to do with fear of failure. Work stress is to do with fearing that you cannot cope, that you will not do a good enough job, be overlooked for promotion and so forth.

When you next feel stressed in a situation ask yourself what you are afraid of.

The goal of mind/body techniques is to activate the relaxation response and reduce the stress response. When you are relaxed, the levels of hormones related to stress are reduced and your immune system is more efficient.

Doctors are now encouraging patients to try mind/body techniques like meditation, yoga and cognitive behavioural therapy to activate the relaxation response. They recognise that sometimes people do not need pills they need to let off steam, talk things through (*to be heard*) as well as physically release tension from the body.

Is relaxation enough?

I believe that whilst relaxation will be a key part of your healing process that there is a lot more involved than just taking time out to relax. You may be unaware that you are holding any tension or blocked energy within your body. I certainly was.

On one occasion before my own healing process, I went for an aromatherapy massage as friends had told me I would enjoy it. I lay on the massage table and relaxed (or so I thought). The aromatherapist mixed some oils and started to massage my body, then stopped and asked me to relax. I told her I already was and she made it clear that I was not and that she would find it hard to get a good result in the time we had. I was so disconnected with my body that I had no idea I was tensing my muscles and also had no idea how to stop it.

We are starting an opening up process, releasing old trapped emotional hurts and feelings. Releasing these after years when they have become pushed down and locked away, allows your body to "give a huge sigh of relief", relax and set about healing. You are going to reconnect with all parts of yourself and we are going to use your sub conscious mind to do it.

Whatever the research says, one thing I know for certain is the effect writing this book had on me. Whilst revisiting my own history I had to put myself back into the situation to be able to write from that perspective. I began to feel very unwell and went down with two colds (*a sign of mental confusion and hurt*). The headaches (*making myself wrong in some way*) also returned as my thoughts went back along some old patterns (*neural pathways*) that no longer hold true for me. My thinking has changed so much it all felt alien, like a previous life experience. I was very glad to finish and use the tools you are learning here to restore balance and harmony.

So why did that happen after I have healed?

Two reasons:

It is all to do with the neural pathways. When we have thoughts over a period of time it is like creating deep set tyre tracks in your brain. The more you activate those thoughts the more entrenched they become and this goes on for years unless you change your thoughts. As those pathways become stronger or deeper I guess you could say you are "in a rut". Once you change your thinking and adapt to a new pathway the old one diminishes with lack of use.

However it is possible to activate it again if you focus your thoughts that way or something occurs that reminds you of it repeatedly. This is true when you seem to react to something out of proportion to what has happened. It has "pushed your buttons" and reminded you of another occasion, activating memory and emotions and taking you down a negative thought pattern (or tyre track).

The Universal Law of Attraction. You have probably heard or read of this universal law, in a nutshell what you focus on grows, what you give out you get back. It is always important to focus on what you want rather than what you do not want. So it is important for YOU not to think about your health problems anymore but to focus on healing and your good health. Your conscious and sub conscious mind will set about bringing what you believe into being.

The difficulty you face when you suddenly discover a health challenge like getting diagnosed with fibroids or any other condition is the immediate shock and then the fear. Suddenly you have entered a whole new alien world where you seem to be under attack from some horrible monster. Wherever you turn you can read or hear other peoples' horror stories of mis-diagnosis or waiting for treatment too long. When you listen to these stories and get the negative spin on your experience you cannot improve, things just seem to get a whole lot worse. It becomes a relief to just hand your body over to a surgeon and let them cut whatever it is out of your body.

Because I have experienced first hand this universal law in action in very positive ways I must admit to getting a little fearful as I was writing and editing this book. Focussing on fibroids and health concerns again seemed risky. However, once I focussed on seeing this as a chance to help others heal the fear left.

We will be accessing your own mind/body link in the meditation and the exercises you are going to do next.

Only go ahead with the next exercise if you have at least 45 minutes free and make sure you have everything you need to hand before you start.

Exercise 4 – Audio Mind Body Link

 # Meditation combined with Non-dominant hand drawing and writing exercises.

Very useful in getting feedback from yourself (your sub-conscious).

To give this a try I suggest you get the materials you need ready on a table close to you.

Materials:
Drawing or writing pad
Coloured pencils, pen

Put on your *Release & Heal CD* tracks 4 and 5 for this exercise and follow directions after the short meditation.
 The only important thing to remember is to use your non-dominant hand for your drawing. That is the opposite hand to the one you usually use to write with. So if you are right handed then you will use your left.

Use any colours you like.

Do not question what comes just let it express itself.

Do not try to control what comes or make something come, remain relaxed with no expectations.

Once you have finished your drawing listen to the audio explanation on track 6.

Exercise 5 – Health Beliefs

Allow at least 30 minutes for this exercise.

Health Beliefs Exercise

Get your notebook out and write the following lists and answer the questions:

List all of your mother's illnesses

List all of your father's illnesses

List all of your illnesses
(regular colds, asthma, chronic conditions etc.)

Do you see a connection?

What do you remember about your childhood illnesses?

What, if anything did you enjoy about being sick as a child?
(extra attention, special food or drinks, no school etc.)

What did you learn from your parents about illness?
(carry on regardless, illness shows weakness, illness allows you to opt out of responsibility etc)

How have you contributed to the state of your health?
(habits, patterns, lack of care etc.)

Would you like your condition to change, if so in what way?

Florence Schovel Shinn says in her book The Game of Life "The body may be renewed and transformed through the spoken word and clear vision, and disease be completely wiped out of the consciousness. The metaphysician knows that all disease has a mental correspondence, and in order to heal the body one must first "heal the soul." The soul is the subconscious mind, and it must be "saved" from wrong thinking".

Having recalled information about your health and attitudes from your childhood it would prove useful for you to check out the metaphysical roots of any health problems you and your family have been experiencing. You can do this free online at: vwww.vitalaffirmations.com check out the healing cards.

There is an exhaustive list of conditions and you will find it fascinating. Note down the affirmations that you see on the website relating to your particular health challenges.

Alternatively go to the library or bookshop and pick up a copy of "Heal Your Body" by Louise L. Hay and you will again find a list to work with.

Why is it important to try and remember how illness was handled when you were a child?

To answer that I will use myself as an example:

I remembered when I did this exercise how, as a child if I was very ill I stopped having to be responsible and could take a break for a little while. I suddenly realised how I had been using this sub consciously in my working life. I would take on more and more work, say yes to extra projects and be the one to work till midnight if required and I would keep going. In the end my body would give me a reason to stop by becoming very ill, too ill to work. This had the desired effect as it gave me what I saw as an acceptable way to say "no" to even more work and take a rest. I have released that pattern of behaviour as I realised that was not serving me. I learned

to say "no" before getting overloaded and to honour my own
boundaries as I learned to love myself more.

You finished that exercise by setting an intention. Writing about
how you want your condition to change. Next I will give you some
suggestions for making easy positive changes to your daily life to
assist your body to heal.

SUMMARY

Next time you feel "stressed" ask yourself what you are fearful of.

Learn to listen to your body's messages. If you feel pain anywhere in
the body stop for a moment and consider what has caused that.

Check out the metaphysical roots of any health problems you may
have had and also those of your family.

Where you have uncovered old belief patterns from your childhood
about illness consider whether or not they really serve you and be
prepared to let them go.

Complete all exercises before moving on.

Body Care & Maintenance

Many of the people I meet are high achievers whether in the workplace, at home or both. They juggle many things and their personal needs, especially their nutritional and health needs, come last. For those who are single, preparing and cooking a proper meal seems like a waste of time. Whatever the reasons, sitting down for a nutritious and relaxing meal is often foregone in favour of food on the run, ready meals and snacks to keep you going.

In order for your body to heal itself you need to give it the materials for the job. Once you get in the habit of eating more healthily it will get easier and snack or sweet cravings will disappear. There are plenty of books, articles and guides for a healthy diet and your diet may already be pretty good but just needs a little tweaking.

Whilst I have never been one to advocate pill popping, if you suspect your eating has been less than healthy get a good quality all round vitamin and mineral supplement just for the short term whilst you adjust your eating habits.

Take the time to read articles, listen to programmes and ask a nutritionist for their ideas, sift them and decide how and what you want to incorporate in your life (by the way I hate the word diet because it has become associated with lack and deprivation and this book is definitely not about that).

Basic Nutritional Guidelines:

Start eating lots of fresh fruits and vegetables (organic is best).

Add in beans, nuts, seeds, whole grains such as brown rice, wheat germ, wheat germ oil, and nutritional yeast. You need the fibre from the fruit, vegetable and whole grains to help waste products travel through the bowel, and keep your whole system working and cleansing effectively. People who do not eat enough fibre tend to be constipated.

Eat diuretic foods, like cucumbers and watermelons, and dark green leafy vegetables to neutralize and flush out toxins.

Avoid drinking caffeine and carbonated sodas.

Avoid concentrated starches like pastries and fatty dairy foods, hormone-laden meats and refined sugars.

Avoid fried and salty foods, especially smoked or preserved.

Avoid white flour and refined foods.

Drink plenty of water every day.

Get in the habit of cooking your own fresh food, generally any "ready-meals" or prepared shop foods or takeaways are of little nutritional value, can be fat laden and contain additives.

Avoid alcohol, no need to completely give it up but be sensible it does not provide anything that your body needs and causes all sorts of stress as your body tries to deal with its toxicity.

There is no need for you to become vegetarian or go macrobiotic unless you really want to or enjoy it.

I have tried the macrobiotic diet and found that it did not suit me at all. I also know a lady who has eaten that way for most of her life and yet still had cancer.

If you severely restrict or change your diet you are going to feel miserable and will not keep going with it. Quality of life is important and enjoying your food is part of that.

Starting today introduce more vegetables and fruit bit by bit.

If you are working, cut down on any sugary or salty snacks you usually eat in the office. Instead, even if it is only once a day replace one chocolate bar with a small pack of unsalted nuts or a handful of sunflower or pumpkin seeds....too much to ask? Then try a cereal bar or piece of fruit. Bananas are very satisfying and very good for you.

Make this easy on yourself. Change white bread for wheatgerm or wholemeal bread. I am sure you can come up with solutions or substitutions of your own that you would feel comfortable with and that would not make you feel like you were denying or punishing yourself. This is not a DIET this is a change to a more natural and healthy way of life. Your body will respond well and you will start to feel good.

It is amazing how if you start with some small changes swapping old habits for new healthier ones, even more changes will take place. For instance reducing sugar intake ultimately reduces sugar cravings as blood sugar levels get more on an even keel and the "absolute need for" chocolate, biscuits and the like reduces dramatically.

In the early stages of doing this, especially if your diet was previously poor, you may struggle and sometimes slip back into old habits. If this happens do not beat yourself up. Focus on the good you are already achieving and will continue to achieve, because as you know what we focus on grows and self criticism just breaks the spirit – how unkind is that?

Exercising your body

If you are already into exercise, brilliant I am preaching to the converted.

For those who are not, the word exercise can conjure up feelings of fear, pain or embarrassment and pictures of sweaty bodies doing aerobics. In truth any time we move or stretch our bodies we are exercising. In order to function effectively our bodies need to be kept in good order. If you are already making changes to your eating habits enabling your body to function more effectively, adding in some moderate exercise will bring beneficial changes far more quickly.

One of the best methods of getting more exercise is just to walk. You do not require any special equipment, leotard or gym membership and with just twenty minutes medium paced walking three times a week your circulation and muscle tone will improve. So use the car less or park it further away from your destination. Take the stairs instead of the lift. Get yourself a step counter (pedometer) and you will see what a difference those small changes will make. The joy of being outside in the sunshine and fresh air brings other benefits and has a positive effect on your mental health. It is worth noting that Vitamin D is made in the skin with the help of sunlight.

I am particularly keen on yoga because it is gentle and calming, it uses the body and mind and is like meditation for the body. They also focus on breathing in yoga. Second to that I am a huge fan of Pilates if you want to tone your body and reshape it. It can be a lot stronger than yoga but again it calms mind and body and is done slowly with awareness at your own pace.

If you enjoy aerobics or gym workouts find a local class and get started. The important thing is to do something and do it regularly. Make it "me time". Once you get into it, feel and see the benefits then you will continue. Taking regular exercise is something that must be incorporated into your life for all your life not just in fits and starts. So make it something that you enjoy (dancing qualifies).

If you are putting off going to a yoga class or similar because you do not like the way your body looks please do not be concerned. I have seen all shapes, sizes and abilities at the classes and the joy is that everyone is concentrating on their own movements and not you.

Breathe

The joy of exercise is that it naturally encourages you to breathe more deeply and increase blood flow to all parts of the body.

Andrew Weil MD (author of 8 Weeks to Optimal Health) states that "conscious breathing is the most important thing we can do for our health, regardless of exercise and diet".

We all have our own reality, what we believe about life, our role and how others will treat or respond to us. This is based on past experience. As a result of life events there can be times when we feel under threat (mentally, emotionally or physically); we may have experienced other people's anger and fear as we grew up. This can change our natural breathing pattern - we can unconsciously start to suppress or hold our breath especially when we believe something bad is about to happen. At the same time as we are limiting our breathing we may be making a limiting decision about life or ourselves e.g. "I am not worth loving"..."people hurt you if they love you"....."I can't do anything right". These decisions keep us safe to ensure the same event will not happen again. Unfortunately, these personal laws, often made as a child without full understanding of what is going on, do not always create harmony in our lives. If we fail to resolve these traumatic events at the time, they can remain in the form of contracted energy (cellular memory). This in turn can result in illness, depression, lack of joy, or aches and pains in the body.

Conscious Breathing is so important that I run Breath-work sessions for my clients. That particular technique is extremely powerful but is not suitable to be done alone. If you have not heard of Breathwork you may have come across Rebirthing. Some years ago "Re-birthing" became very popular and fashionable as a therapy with the work of Leonard Orr. Since then many others have developed various techniques and it is no longer necessary to set out to go through the re-birthing experience to enjoy the benefits from working on your breathing. Techniques like Transformational and Healing or Conscious Breathwork allow an individual to choose issues they would like to work on and to take it at their own pace with the guidance of a practitioner. They have also brought in an element of spirituality for those wishing to work on this aspect of their lives.

Even without attending workshops or Breath sessions you can become aware of your breathing patterns and how they change under differing circumstances. As a simple example; a friend of mine discovered that he holds his breath when concentrating on computer work. He had never really noticed this or the stress that it caused his body, now that he is aware of it, when he notices it coming on he just breathes steadily throughout his work, continuing to feed the body/brain with the oxygen it needs to operate effectively and in a more relaxed mode.

If you are used to meditating then you will be aware of how the breathing quietens and slows down when you are relaxed and meditating and the wonderful feeling of calm that comes from that. Just take the time right now to notice how your body is feeling, are there areas of tension? Are you breathing fully i.e down into the abdomen or just in your upper chest?

As most people are shallow breathers, and some of us tend to hold our stomachs in, I am asking you to regularly scan your body for tension and notice how you are breathing. Whenever you can take a moment to focus on your breath, relax the body and breathe in fully. By that I mean so that your stomach balloons a little as you breathe in and collapses again as you completely exhale. Don't hold your breath and do not force it.

My Own Personal Breathing Experience

As with all practical things you can read or hear about them but if you want to benefit from them you have to actually try it. I was a little nervous when I first went to a breath workshop as I was unsure quite how the whole thing would work.

As I settled down on my mat for a session and tried to relax whilst breathing intensely, I wondered "what on earth am I doing here?" Some time passed and I began to hear others around me who seemed to be experiencing all sorts of emotions and insights and yet here I was wondering "am I doing it right?"

Eventually I stopped worrying, decided that this was just going to be like a meditation and relaxed. As soon as I gave up trying, suddenly I found myself overcome with some intense emotions which had been sparked by the sound of a child laughing. It was close to the end of the first session and so I was encouraged to "let it go for now" and bring my attention back to the room. However, the strength of feeling and curiosity it had generated in me were not so easy to let go of and I felt very sad.

In the afternoon I had another session and suddenly found the insight I was looking for. As a child I had been extremely frightened on at least one occasion by an individual close to me. I can only have been around five or six years old. as I look back as an adult the situation I recalled was not so terrible but of course to a small child it was petrifying and had caused me to stay locked in that fear, colouring my adult judgement on relationships.

The joy of Breathwork is that the practitioner guides you through this process and I was able to literally breathe the fear away, it released a pain in my back and my legs and I felt like a burden had been lifted. As it happens I needed another two sessions to really get to the bottom of all that I had been holding onto.

I have since had some very "blissful" experiences with breathwork. However, from my own personal experience I can tell you that it can be a little scary, as although you set your intention for the session you do not always know what will pop up. But, it is also exciting, I do know that it is a rich learning experience and has brought release and a shift in my life which had not been brought about by other techniques I have tried.

Now, following my own training, as I guide people through their sessions I feel so privileged to share in their experiences. I am amazed at the kind of things that can happen to us through life and the way in which we survive and grow. It is both fascinating and sad that these events colour and determine how we view life. People carry heavy loads sometimes and to see them "blow those away" is wonderful.

You cannot always tell by looking at someone what their life story is. So treat those around you lovingly and gently. Also know that if you are thinking of trying this or other techniques trust your judgement. If it does not sound or feel right for you then leave it alone. You will instinctively be drawn to what is right for you when the right opportunity and time arises.

Working with your breath will certainly assist the healing process. It is worth looking for a local Breath-work practitioner, preferably someone who does not focus on re-birthing but deals more with healing or transformational breath-work. If this isn't possible check my website for other resources that give you something you can try by yourself *(see resources)*.

SUMMARY

Give your body the premium fuel it needs. Upgrade your nutrition where necessary. Eat fresh foods and take advice from a nutritionist or read up on what would best suit your body. Drink plenty of water.

Take regular exercise, at the very least walking and ensure you step up the pace from time to time to tone the cardiovascular system.

Breathe in a relaxed and full fashion. Regularly check how you are breathing.

Make some changes today no matter how small.

Start Using Positive Affirmations

Every thought and statement you make is an affirmation. You are affirming what you believe.

So are your thoughts and words positive or negative?

Unsure?

Catch your next thought (not always easy) and see. Notice what is said in the next conversation with your friends. Are you commiserating with each other about how stressed, busy, tired you are, how someone always lets you down?
Maybe you discuss how good things do not happen to you or will probably go wrong, how if it is not one thing then it's another?

These are all negative words that reflect your thinking and will be reflected in your continuing life experience.

The good news is that positive affirmations assist your body to relax and feel supported and can be effectively used in the process of change to replace negative self speak i.e. the negative thoughts that go through your mind (and affect your body) like "I never get anything right" or "no-one is ever going to love me" or "this health problem will not go away".

To replace those statements you would use affirmations like "I am effective and can do anything I want to"…and "I am loving and lovable" or "I now attract the perfect loving partner" and "I am in perfect health" or "I am healthy, healed and whole".

You will have noticed that the affirmations are always positive, present tense and personal. You state them as you want your life to be and as though it already is that way.

Why?

The subconscious mind is an amazing creation and can take things quite literally, so if you state that "I want to be effective" it will note that and put it aside as something you want in the future. As you know tomorrow never comes so you will not get it.

If on the other hand you say "I am effective" then your sub conscious mind acts on that, adopts those characteristics and achieves it. So you can probably see that if you do not want illness in your life then affirming that you will get rid of this illness will only put that as something for the future. Dis-ease and illness should not be mentioned at all. The affirmation to use is "I am healthy, healed and whole". Focus on the desired outcome and speak and think as if it is already true.

When you first start doing this it does not feel right or true, it can feel distinctly odd and silly. That is a natural and extremely common reaction. But it really is worth persevering.

You will start to notice as you become more aware of your thoughts the negative messages that pop up. So for example if you were to say to yourself "I am beautiful and everybody loves me" you might hear your inner critic say "yeah right in your dreams".

These negative thoughts or affirmations are useful to be aware of as they are old tapes playing in your head. Usually they are things that have been said or conveyed to you by people or experiences that have impacted your life. Then they have been stored away to continue replaying day after day.
These are the very messages we want to replace. Where possible note them down in your notebook and then convert them into positive affirmations to speed up the process.

For instance if when I said to myself "I am beautiful" I heard in my head "you would be if you didn't look so old" then I would affirm "I am energetic, youthful and vibrant and my appearance reflects this".

Visualisation

Visualisation is a very useful tool for making changes more quickly and increasing your personal power. It brings even more power to your affirmations when you combine the two and attach as much detail as possible.

Emotions and feelings really add to the overall reality of whatever it is you wish to bring into your life. Athletes have known that this technique works for years. Quite often trainers will get Olympic contenders to visualise themselves winning the race or tournament. They have been using it in Cancer treatment centres, getting patients to visualise their body's natural defence system fighting or eradicating the cancer cells. Personally I do not like the thought of war taking place inside my body. I prefer to see any black areas surrounded by light and absorbed into the light. You might wish to visualise a beautiful, bright cleansing light flowing through your whole body and see your body glow as it cleanses and heals all areas.

The important thing here is to find images that work and feel right for you.

Visualising yourself as happy, healed and whole is the goal, so use images, thoughts and feelings that support this.

Examples of Affirmations

Here are some examples of affirmations to work with daily just read them through:

I love and accept myself exactly as I am

I nurture and support myself

I know that I am always doing the best I can

I trust myself

I deserve love

I am worth loving

I am a marvellous and beautiful creation

I am beautiful and everybody loves me

I am a vibrant, healthy, creative being

I am loved and appreciated for the wonderful person I am

I am beautiful and loving inside and out

People love to be around me

My body is perfect, healthy, healed and whole

I love and embrace my femininity/masculinity

I now choose to love myself

If you struggled to even read the affirmations then start with "I now commit to learning to love myself" or "I am willing to start thinking about loving myself". Now as you will appreciate from what I have said before this will keep things in the future so this is a temporary measure. But just by starting to accept that you may be able to do this, opens the possibilities up to you.

So if that is the case for you then you can start with those less direct affirmations initially and then after a day or two of working with them move on to the direct present tense ones such as "I love and accept myself exactly as I am".

In order to promote this way of thinking continue straight on with the next exercise.

Exercise 6 – Health Affirmations

Writing an affirmation can intensify its power. In your notebook write one positive affirmation about your health 20 times. Create your own or choose one of the following:

My healing is already in process
I listen with love to my body's messages.
My health is radiant, vibrant and dynamic now.
I am grateful for my perfect health.
I deserve good health.

Use the Mirror to empower your affirmations.

Doing your affirmations whilst looking in the mirror gives them more weight and speeds up the process.

Ladies I know that we all have to look in the mirror several times a day anyway, but do you ever look yourself in the eyes and tell yourself "I love and accept myself exactly as I am"? It can be quite hard to do but will bring excellent results if maintained over a period of time. Do not under estimate the power of positive thinking.

Gentlemen, whilst you may not look in the mirror as often as the ladies you can still take the time to do this. Especially whilst brushing your teeth, combing your hair or shaving (with caution).

The important thing is to do it whenever you look in the mirror as that makes it easy to achieve quick results. Any additional dedicated mirror/affirmation work is a huge bonus.

If you find yourself criticising others on a regular basis then I guarantee that you are doing far worse to yourself inside. Stop all criticism. I know that you would never say a fraction of the things to someone else that you beat yourself up with, so make a conscious decision to stop it now.

Exercise 7 – Mirror Work

Right now find a large hand mirror or stand in front of a wall mirror, with a notebook and pen to hand.

As you look yourself in the eyes say "I love and accept you just as you are".

How difficult was that?

Were you actually able to say it whilst looking yourself in the eye?

Was it uncomfortable?

Try again and this time say to yourself "I could love myself more if….." and listen to what thoughts come up in your mind. Say it several times and each time jot down what thoughts come back.

After a few minutes take the time to convert those negative messages into written positive affirmations. So for example if I got the message "…if you did not look so ugly" I would change it to "I am beautiful" and I might also add "and everybody loves me".

Like meditation I feel very strongly about using positive affirmations regularly and consistently in your life. It gets easier the more you practice. The more resistance you feel to doing them the more you need to. It can help to do them with the "Heartfelt" CD (*see resources*).

Exercise 8 – Loving and Accepting Your Body

Make sure you have enough time to yourself, and that you are in a warm secure room with a full length mirror. Stand in front of the mirror without any clothes on. Look at yourself, yes I know this is probably way outside your comfort zone.

In the same way as the previous exercise just notice what negative messages come up in your mind.

As you now look at yourself start to marvel at how amazing the human body is with its myriad of functions that it performs ceaselessly day and night. The way it accommodates the pressures we put on it. Remember the fact that we are all unique and have different features.

Take particular time over any areas of your body you dislike. Gently touch those parts and appreciate how you need them as part of the whole. You may notice that these areas feel colder than other parts of the body.

Take time over this and keep affirming "I love and appreciate my body".

When you have finished sit for 5 or 10 minutes and convert any negative messages you received into positive affirmations, write them down. Use these affirmations or just stick with the loving one if that is easier. Put your list of affirmations somewhere you will see it regularly (e.g. in your underwear draw).

SUMMARY

Visualise yourself as a healthy person right now. Add feeling and emotion to the positive affirmations you use to super charge them.

Use the mirror to do your daily affirmations.

Acknowledge and appreciate all parts of your body (even the bits you feel are less than perfect). Treat your body lovingly maybe using a luxurious body lotion.

Make sure you have completed all exercises before moving on.

Releasing the Past

As you continue to practice your meditation, using positive affirmations and working through this book, you are becoming more aware of sub-conscious patterns of behaviour and beliefs.

Ultimately you want to release the conditions that have contributed to your current health and allow the bodies own natural healing intelligence to take over. A good affirmation here would be "I now choose to release the patterns of behaviour and beliefs in me that have contributed to this condition".

At some time everyone experiences resentment, bitterness, anger, hatred, and other emotions from people and situations that have occurred in their life. These are natural emotions and problems only start to arise when these emotions are held onto.

Seemingly terrible things do happen, and people can be cruel and unkind, but one thing is certain, when people stay locked in these emotions unwilling to forgive, they are the only ones that suffer. Being trapped like this is a bit like making a huge pot of stew to last you a life time and then reheating it every day to serve up for lunch. Knowing how unhealthy, unappetising and down right disgusting that would be, you would not dream of doing such a thing. Yet you are doing it emotionally everyday, reliving or suffering from something that was created years ago.

Imagine now putting that old stew pot into the sink to clean. It has become so encrusted with burned on crud it seems like an impossible job. But left in warm water with some detergent to soak, bit by bit the crud starts to soften and soon comes off easily with a little elbow grease. That is what you are in the process of doing right now. The exercises we have been and continue to do, are gently lifting off those layers of old conditioning that no longer serve you making it easy to bring about lasting positive change. I will shortly show you some powerful releasing and clearing techniques to enable you to "get that pot clean even quicker" and get rid of what you may be holding on to.

Anger releasing

 If any one tells me "I never get angry" then I am usually concerned that they have lost touch with their feelings or emotions.

This can happen for many reasons. One of the most common is if they have experienced the negative effects of extreme anger and violent behaviour growing up. As a result they try to avoid it in adulthood and feel very uncomfortable and fearful if people start to get angry. They are quite often pacifiers and people pleasers. There are also many who were brought up in families where getting angry was totally unacceptable behaviour.

Unfortunately on the face of it whilst everything looks calm there is damage being created inside. Resentment, fear and anger can build up and create dis-ease in the body if it is not released in a safe and appropriate way. As they deny and push down all of these "dangerous" or "unacceptable" feelings over a long period they become disconnected within themselves.

Many women find that they are more likely to cry than get angry. Whilst not ideal this is still a way in which your body is trying to release.

In my case as I grew up I saw my Mother keep everything inside until she reached bursting point and then totally flip and lose control, which was noisy and scary. My Father seemed more controlled and the more my Mother got mad the more quiet he got, ignoring her behaviour. This as you have probably guessed fuelled my Mothers' anger, she would push and push him trying to get a reaction. Being the youngest I watched what everybody did and soon recognised the signs that my mother was starting to get angry and did everything I could to keep her calm and avoid the nuclear explosion that would come.

As time went by I made the decision that completely losing control did not get you what you want. I developed my own style. As a people watcher I stored away bits of information on those around me. I knew what buttons to press and the comments to make that would cut like a knife. I never needed to get loud or "nuts" if you upset me I could annihilate you with a single sentence and leave you devastated.

Friends and colleagues congratulated me for being able to say the perfect thing at the time rather than coming up with it later after the other person had gone. What they did not realise was the damage it caused to myself and the others. You cannot take back what you have said. Walking away knowing I had hurt someone did not make me feel good and although I seemed calm and in control it would take hours to calm down and let it go afterwards.

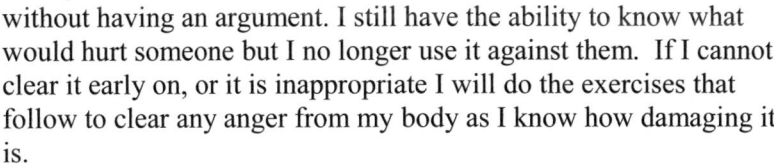

Thankfully I have learned a new way and I no longer use that technique. Once I cleared out the real cause of my anger, the reasons why others could push my buttons, I no longer reacted so strongly. Now, if appropriate when someone does or says something that feels wrong I will tell them so and clear the air without having an argument. I still have the ability to know what would hurt someone but I no longer use it against them. If I cannot clear it early on, or it is inappropriate I will do the exercises that follow to clear any anger from my body as I know how damaging it is.

If you find yourself flying off the handle with people over seemingly small events then there is more going on underneath (usually old

anger) and it is very important you find safe and appropriate ways of dealing with it.

Adrenalin is released into our systems when we get stressed, excited, feel threatened or fearful. This needs to be released. Men often find going for a run really useful here or using the punch bag in the gym.

Let's get started doing something practical to release old emotions, especially anger.

Exercise 9 – Releasing Old Emotions

Before starting this two part exercise please make sure you have time to complete it, allow at least 40 minutes. Both parts have to be completed at the same session.

We want to release old emotions that keep us stuck in old patterns. These will not only include anger, but also resentment, guilt, and fear. Some of us may not have had very good models for expressing and releasing these emotions as we grew up, so our bodies literally store these emotions until they are expressed.

A key to healing is being aware of stored feelings, expressing them, and releasing them. Think for a moment about how these emotions, especially anger, were handled when you were growing up? How do you handle them now?

Part 1 - Written mental exercise

Get a separate piece of paper to write on. You'll be tearing it up and throwing it away later. We're going to do a written awareness exercise.

As you're doing this exercise, be careful not to censor yourself. Emotions don't have to make sense. It's OK to feel and acknowledge the emotions you have.

Have you ever noticed that you tend to get angriest at the people you love the most? This is normal, as the ones close to us really know how to push our buttons, we have higher expectations of them but also quite often (unless an abusive partner) they are the safest to be angry with. A stranger would not tolerate that kind of behaviour.

Close your eyes and take a deep breath. Allow your body to relax. Tell yourself that you are ready and willing to become aware of the emotions you have been holding that are keeping you stuck, and you are ready to let them go.

Stay in that inner-directed space, but now open your eyes and complete the following sentence:

I feel angry at (name the person or situation)................

Because...........

Finish that sentence 3 different times. It might be the same person or a different person each time. (Repeat: I feel angry at....because......)

Where do you feel that anger in your body? Just be aware.

Now finish this sentence:

I feel guilty because........

Finish that 3 times. Where do you feel the guilt in your body? Just notice where it is.

Now finish the sentence:

I feel fear that.................

Finish that sentence 3 times.

Where in your body do you feel the fear?

Part 2 - Practical Anger Releasing Exercise

If you are at home, with no one around and can be by yourself for about twenty minutes then the following is a useful method for both men and women:

Go into the bedroom, take off your shoes (and any jewellery) and then jump up and down lifting feet off the floor and swinging your arms whilst shouting "yes, no, get off my back" and do that three times.

Then take a very short breather and do it again three times. Do not hold back, make it loud and lively, like a child having a tantrum.

Following straight on from that, kneel on the floor with several pillows and punch them hard until you feel the release and start to tire. Alternatively you could punch the mattress on your bed. Allow whatever feelings that come up to flow out, this is one of those times when it is best to disengage your brain and not try to work out what is coming up and why. The important thing here is just to release.

Now start to name the people you wrote about in the previous exercises and address them and what they have done to you, how it made you feel etc. out loud whilst punching the pillows or mattress.

Address your fears and guilt and get this stuff out of your system.

There is no one around, no one to judge what you are expressing so swear if you want to. Really get mad and feel the energy build and release. No need to try and be fair on the person in question this is just for you.

Do not be concerned if anger is coming out but you do not know who or what it is to do with. Just go with it.

Now close your eyes and take a deep breath.

Are you willing to forgive those you have been angry with and resentful toward?

No? Why not? Express why not, you have a right to all your own emotions, you have a right to be angry so punch the pillows some more.

Yes? Then imagine telling each one you forgive them.

And if you're not ready to do that, that's OK.

Are you ready to forgive yourself? Let go of the guilt. You were truly doing the best you could at the time, and so was everyone else.

Be gentle with your fear. Be aware of the places in your body where you felt these different emotions.

Take a VERY deep breath, and then blow it out, imagining that you are releasing these emotions from your body. Do this three times. Then take a few gentle breaths. Give yourself a big hug.

How did it feel to let go of the anger, guilt, and fear?

Does your body feel lighter?

Get your piece of paper, tear it up and throw it away to symbolize the clearing and letting go.

I find the above exercise particularly useful if I suddenly find that I feel uncomfortable in my body. For me this is like a feeling in my guts or stomach area and usually happens if I have heard something that disturbs me or if something has pushed my buttons but I am unsure what.

Manage your own anger

If you find your anger is disproportionate to the current event, look to past events or traumas. If you do not feel anger when most would, then consider why you have become so disconnected from your feelings and emotions.

It is very important to manage your own anger appropriately for the safety of yourself and others and in particular if you have children.

Being honest about your true feelings and not holding things back (allowing them to build) helps a good deal. But there is also a need to examine where the anger is coming from. In the example that Dr. Northrup gave (*page 31*), Gina got angry when her brother died but did not express it saying she was "25 years old". Suggesting that to have such feelings was wrong or childish. That belief will have come from an earlier time. However, once she allowed herself to feel it and release it her healing took place. She now knows how damaging it can be to hold onto old hurt, resentment and anger.

When you have really released such emotions then you can get to a place of forgiveness. This is not always easy, but frees the soul and allows love to flow in.

Forgiveness is a powerful healing tool, it does not condone what happened, just releases the individual from continuing to be a victim.

You will find some people or situations easy to forgive but with others it will seem almost impossible. It is necessary to get the anger and pain released first. Moving too quickly to a place of forgiveness can stop the clearing process.

Exercise 10 – Audio Anger releasing meditation

Listen to the Anger releasing meditation, track 7 on your *Release &
Heal CD.*

If you have not done the releasing exercises yet – why not? Is their
some resistance? Are you stuck in a place of self-righteous
resentment?

Do the exercises, it is not necessary to deal with everything that
needs releasing in one go but you do need to start somewhere. Work
on that before moving onto the forgiveness exercises.

Forgiveness

Forgiveness is an essential element of learning to love yourself and releasing all the old anger, hurt and resentment you may have locked away inside.

So many times people feel they have a right to be angry or bear a grudge because someone has done something so terrible to them many years ago.

Firstly you have a right to all your feelings and emotions. However, I can assure you that if you hold onto them long after the event has taken place they will cause dis-ease within your body and you are the one who will suffer yet again. The set of beliefs and negative thoughts that come from this will then colour your view of life and your expectations of it.

Forgiving someone does not mean condoning bad behaviour; it means moving on and not getting stuck in the past. It means releasing yourself from further torment and takes the power of that event or person away.

Quite often the most difficult person to forgive is ourselves. We feel we may have deserved something, done something wrong or allowed something to happen. Again we remain stuck with negative thoughts and beliefs about ourselves.

The greatest gift you can give yourself is to forgive everyone, including yourself, release the past and open the doors to love and freedom.

How?

We have already done some work on releasing anger, guilt and fear and in that last audio exercise we did some forgiveness work. The next exercise is one you can do with a trusted friend or partner, but only if it feels comfortable for both of you. If you do not have someone else to do this with then repeat the previous audio exercise and keep changing the person you are confronting or create your own visualisation until you have cleared out all the people you may be angry or upset with. Alternatively use the whole of the "Heartfelt" CD (details in resources).

Exercise 11 – Forgiveness

If you have a trusted friend with whom you could share an exercise use the previous audio as above then immediately sit facing your partner. Take each others hands and decide who will go first. Then name someone and start with for example "Mum I forgive you for....." and say all the things you have been holding inside, let out all the hurts and resentment, all the things that have caused you pain.

When you have finished your partner then says "Thank you and I set you free" and nothing else.

This is not the time to start a conversation about what you have said just move on to the next person you need to forgive and if you are that person then good. Yes strange as it may seem you can use this exercise to forgive yourself.

Continue doing this until you have exhausted your list for now and then let your partner do the same.

It helps for you both to have your eyes closed when you do this. I must re-emphasise that it is important you do not get involved in a discussion with your partner about why you have said what you said and whether or not it is fair and reasonable. No judgement must be made by either of you.

Exercise 12 - Angel letters

These are a wonderful way of releasing any old hurt, anger or issues of any kind with someone you would not be able to talk with i.e. someone who has died, is not in contact or where it might cause more friction to talk it out face to face.

Use the example below as a template. Please give it a try, I cannot count the number of times participants from my workshops have come back to tell me the great results they have had with this.

Whether or not you believe in angels does not matter. This is your higher self (the self not bogged down with the day to day squabbles and trials of life) talking to the higher self of the other person involved.

You may find that you get very quick results from this but do not attach any outcome to it just allow it to be released for delivery. You do not have to believe in it, put it to the test now. Let me give you a real life example:

A lady on one of my workshops having finished doing her forgiveness work with a partner was given the task of writing an angel letter. She did not take it too seriously but decided to use it on someone who upset her at her previous place of work.

He had made life unpleasant and contributed greatly to her decision to leave the job and she had not seen him since (over a year).

She wrote down all her anger and upset and explained how she had felt about him and what he had done.

Then (as you can see from the template below) she wrote about the good that came out of her experience with him. There is always a lesson or something good from all experiences, in this case it had prompted her to make a move that she probably should have made before and led onto a much better and happier job.

She completed the letter, folded it up and put it away. I told her she would know if and when it had been delivered.

She left the workshop, met up with her husband and they decided to take a walk and go for a drink (something they did not do regularly). As soon as she walked into the pub she saw the very guy she had written her letter to.

Not wishing to attract his attention they sat off to the side quietly.

Eventually he spotted her and walked right over to her saying "I am so glad to see you, I never got a chance to speak to you after you left and I wanted to apologise for what happened between us".

As you can imagine she was completely taken aback, rushed home and telephoned me.

Before this, if I told her this could have happened she would have laughed at me and said "you do not know him". She like others could not get over how quickly and apparently miraculously things can change.

Give it a try.

An Angel letter to the Higher Self of

....

Carried in love by the Angels/ my higher self

Dear ....

(Put here your feelings about your experiences together which may have caused dis-ease between you).

(Put here the good things that have happened between you, or details of what you have learned from the difficult experiences)

I bless you and release you to your higher good.

The spirit in me forgives you for all the anger and sorrow that has been between us. The spirit in you forgives me for all the anger and sorrow that has been between us, now and forever.

In the spirit of love,

Signed ....

This letter is now carried to its destination by the Angels/my higher self for the good of all concerned.

(Now fold the letter, address it to the person or situation concerned and put it in a special place where no one else will find it, for up to 48 hours. You will know when it has been sent! Burn or throw away the letter after it has gone).

SUMMARY

Release the past and old emotions in a safe but effective way. Use the affirmation "I now choose to release the patterns of behaviour and beliefs in me that have contributed to this condition".

Get in touch with your old anger or deal with new anger by doing the practical exercises and techniques from this section. Come back and do them again whenever you feel the need. This is an ongoing process.

Express your needs and views to others when and where appropriate calmly, do not bottle things up.

Use angel letters regularly as a gentle way to keep up the clearing process.

Do not move on without doing all the exercises in this section.

Finding ways to support yourself

Go with the flow

Now is a good time to stop and consider again what your current needs are to help you get through the changes that are taking place. This is an important time, make it as easy on yourself as possible. The following are some suggestions to assist you.

Learning to Accept Help.

When friends, family or others offer help or assistance of whatever kind, smile and say "yes please!"

We all need help or company sometimes and yet we put barriers in the way.

Someone offers us something and we go through a whole mental process of working out why or how it will put us in their debt or be more trouble than it is worth. We may even think "they don't really mean it". That last thought has more to do with us than the other person.

It makes people feel good about themselves when their help is gratefully received. You may have experienced this yourself. How often have you helped someone and then seen the difference it has made?

You do not know what goes on in the mind of anyone else. Do not make decisions based on what you believe someone else is thinking.

Giving and receiving are two sides of the same coin and can be enjoyed equally.

Whilst we are on the subject, never offer help or do something for someone if you do not want to do it, it comes from the wrong place. Always give with a good heart, easily and happily and if you cannot then do not. If you give begrudgingly it diminishes you and the receiver equally. It also builds up resentment in you that will eventually cause physical symptoms and we have already covered all that.

Accept that we all make mistakes

As human beings, we learn by trial, error and success. Making mistakes is a normal part of development.

On the other hand when we keep making the same mistakes over and over then we have to know that on some level all is not well with us. It may be that our old negative belief system is sabotaging us in our efforts. If this has been true for you in the past then as you have been working through this process you may have already identified some patterns.

However, when you are on your journey of self discovery and growth, know that from time to time you will make mistakes and seem to go backwards. This is a very important time for you, the mistake does not matter it is just some old pattern of behaviour that is in the process of being released.

The important thing is not to get it out of proportion and start the old negative self speak like "I knew you wouldn't be able to do it", "your still the same, nothing changes".

Be kind to yourself, acknowledge that you are still learning and that you are improving and finding it so much easier. You are doing really well.

Forgive yourself for whatever the slip is and accept that you are moving on in wonderful ways. Then continue with all the wonderful positive work that you are doing.

Allow the changes to unfold.

Do not try to make loads of changes to yourself at this time. Accept that there is a process happening and unfolding within you that is starting to show in your outward appearance and the way you behave.

Undertaking fad diets (denying yourself something) or trying to "correct" something you do not like about yourself is detrimental and again will sabotage what you are doing.

You are travelling to a place where you love and accept yourself exactly as you are and from that place any changes that need to happen will do so easily and effortlessly, so stop undermining yourself.

Establish and honour your boundaries.

Many of us have people around us in our lives who take our energy and make us feel deflated after we have seen or spoken with them.

If you have people like this around you start setting your own boundaries. If you do not feel like being burdened or dumped on by their "stuff" then don't be rude but make yourself less available and use the word "NO".

It is particularly easy if it is a friend who telephones at awkward times or keeps you on the telephone listening to all their problems. For example you can say that you no longer answer the telephone after seven o'clock now because you want to relax, do something with the kids, read, study whatever it is you enjoy doing.

Stick with this for several weeks. Alternatively use an answer-phone, or caller identifier, until everyone just accepts it.

Avoid watching the news

Especially in the evening avoid watching the news or violent films and documentaries. These will not bring you joy, in fact they will send you to bed with horrible, negative images focusing on the worst aspects of human nature and will not make for a good nights sleep.

Make it a rule to read something positive before turning out your light and going to sleep. Positive affirmations are brilliant.

There follows a set of positive affirmations created by Louise Hay and presented in her book "You Can Heal Your Life". Use it nightly for the next week last thing before you turn the light out and notice if it makes any difference.

Loving Treatment

Deep at the centre of my being there is an infinite well of love. I now allow this love to flow to the surface. It fills my heart, my body, my mind, my consciousness, my very being, and radiates out from me in all directions and returns to me multiplied. The more love I use and give, the more I have to give, the supply is endless. The use of love makes me feel good; it is an expression of my inner joy. I love myself, therefore I take loving care of my body. I lovingly feed it nourishing food and beverages. I lovingly groom it and dress it and my body lovingly responds to me with vibrant health and energy. I love myself, therefore I provide for myself a comfortable home, one that fills all my needs and is a pleasure to be in. I fill the rooms with the vibration of love so that all who enter, myself included, will feel this love and be nourished by it. I love myself, therefore I work at a job that I truly enjoy doing, one that uses all my talents and abilities, working with and for people that I love and love me, and earning a good income. I love myself, therefore, I behave in a loving way to all people for I know that that which I give out returns to me multiplied. I only attract loving people in my world for they are a mirror of what I am. I love myself, therefore I forgive and totally release the past and all past experiences and I am free. I love myself, therefore I love totally in the now, experiencing each moment as good and knowing that my future is bright, and joyous and secure, for I am a beloved child of the universe and the universe lovingly takes care of me now and forever more. And so it is. *(Louise L..Hay)*

Exercise 13 - Treat Yourself.

Take time to recall and list all the various activities you love, especially the ones that you feel are indulgent.
Trusting your own inner wisdom and connecting with your inner-self is a very important part of loving yourself and manifesting a life you love.

Do the exercise below, think in terms of music you like to hear; films that you enjoy and bring back happy memories or make you feel uplifted; friends that make you laugh when you call or see them; walks; silk pyjamas; aromatic bubbly baths; clean sheets; painting; reading etc.

One of the ways to stay in touch with yourself and build trust is nurturing your body and soul with "little things".

List 5 examples of ways in which you might nurture your body and soul under each topic below.

5 x Sensual things (e.g. wearing silk pyjamas, aromatherapy):

5 x Visual/audio things (e.g. sunsets, favourite film, particular music):

5 x Activities (e.g. game of squash, tea with a friend, long walk in the country):

Now when you have your list decide that you will do at least one of those things today and another by the end of the week. Regularly check your list and fit in even more things that bring you joy, especially sensuous things. Do not move on until you have scheduled in the above.

Gratitude

As part of loving yourself and to bring good things into your life it pays to be grateful for the good you already have. Yes you do have good in your life already. You are alive and each new day is a new chance to live, love, share, care and see the beauty around you. That is quite apart from all the wonderful things, people and places we have and encounter everyday.

The simplest analogy I can give for the universal principle here is to liken it to a child who is given a gift and just throws it away without seeing any of the possibilities or joy of it. Taking the attitude that it is not the colour they wanted or the toy they thought they should have. No-one would want to buy gifts for such a child again.

No matter what your life is like there are always things to be grateful for from being alive and having the chance to make a difference, right down to the cup of tea or cocoa in your hand that warms and comforts you.

Exercise 14

One of the best methods for practising gratitude I have found so far is the Gratitude Journal.

You can buy special books for this but they are not necessary. Just find a simple textbook or pad and keep it together with a pen alongside your bed.

Each night before going to sleep write five things you are grateful for today. They can be as basic as someone making you a cup of coffee in the office to having won the lottery.

When you make this a regular event it focuses your mind on the positive things in your life. Although when you start you may find it difficult very quickly you will start finding more and more things to add to your list. You will find yourself writing far more than you ever imagined. Follow this by reading the "Loving Treatment" and then off to sleep.

SUMMARY

Accept help.

Accept that we all make mistakes, that is how we learn.

Allow the changes to unfold naturally.

Establish and honour your boundaries.

Avoid watching the news and violent films in the evening.

Write at least 5 things you are grateful for that day in your gratitude journal and read the "Loving Treatment" last thing at night, every night.

Exercise 15 – Have a Clear Out   (Feng Shui for the Soul)

One way of physically assisting the process of mental and emotional clearing is to clear the clutter in your living space. Most of us have areas or cupboards which are untidy or just crammed full of "stuff". Some of us have whole rooms that store our junk. It makes you feel tired just to look at it or even think about it.

If this is true for you, when you clear those areas several things happen:

- You stop feeling tired or overwhelmed when you look at or think of those areas.

- You gain more free space.

- You allow air and energy to flow in those areas.

- You feel good for having tackled these tasks.

- There is a feeling of facing things, releasing and letting go.

- You gain a sense of control.

This kind of physical clearing assists with the mental processes you are going through right now. Use affirmations at the same time like "as I clear each space I feel the negativity leaving my body and mind allowing the light to shine in".

Before you start remember to always do your clearing in manageable chunks when you have enough time.

For the purposes of this exercise pick one drawer or a small cupboard to clear. Have three large plastic bags or boxes to hand and a rubbish bin. Set one bag aside for things you want to keep, the next for things to recycle to the charity shop or friends and the last for items you no longer want and could sell. Obviously anything else goes in the bin.

Now comes the process:

Empty the area to be cleared completely and clean it. Once cleaned start to look at each item that you have pulled out. If you want to keep it then it goes back in. If it does not belong in this location it is put in the "keeping box". You can find a home for it after you have completed clearing this area.

Anything broken or past its sell by date can be thrown in the rubbish bin. Ladies, make-up does not keep forever (and that includes nail varnish) you do not want something that contains bacteria or is degenerating, on your skin. If you liked the product you would have used it up by now so bin it.

Items which are too good to throw out but that you no longer want, can be recycled or sold and can be put into the appropriate bag.

With clothing if you have not worn it in the last year then you probably never will so pass it on to someone else and make space for something new. If you decide to keep it make sure that it is clean and in good condition when you return it, otherwise put it in the laundry basket and/or mend it.

Continue until everything is back in the drawer/cupboard in one of the bags or the bin.Now empty the bin, take the bags to their destinations i.e. recycling to charity shop, friends, ebay or a similar sales outlet. Do not put the bags away somewhere else, deal with them or your work will have been wasted.

Hanging onto anything that you do not love or that doesn't serve you speaks of lack. Sometimes we hold onto things that were expensive even though we never wear or use them because we invested so much in them. Release them to someone else who can enjoy them. Know that now you have created space other more wonderful things can come into your life.

This process can also have a positive effect on your love life if you have split from a partner.

One lady who came to me had been holding onto all the clothes and personal possessions of her old fiancé who died some years back. A young woman in her early twenties, she had bags and boxes of clutter that she could not bear to look at but felt she could not throw away. She feared that he would think she was trying to forget him. After years of being alone and feeling sad she started working on loving herself and one day woke up deciding to "clear the clutter". It took a whole day but she sorted and cleared, giving mementos to his friends and family, keeping treasured items, recycling his clothes and regaining her own living space. She contacted me very excited and energised and feeling so much lighter. Sure enough, having created a space she shortly afterwards found a new loving relationship. Understandably, no man would have felt comfortable surrounded by another mans belongings in every cupboard and room (dead or not). She still has the love and memories in her heart and found she no longer needed bags and boxes of his stuff.

Once you get into it you may find yourself clearing and organising more and more areas because there is such a sense of achievement and it makes your daily life so much easier. Clutter around you indicates issues like mental confusion and being stuck in some way. As you clear away you are assisting your internal clearing process. You will feel more energised and your living space will improve dramatically.

Relationships

We have been working on changing the relationship you have with yourself to a more loving one. Now let's examine your other relationships.

What a huge topic this is, I could write a whole book on it. Most of the time when we are talking about our relationships, we mean those intimate ones with a significant other. However, relationships abound in our lives. They range from almost unnoticed (for example the woman at the till in the local shop or the milkman) through familial to intimate (lover/husband/wife). All relationships provide us with opportunities to learn about ourselves, grow spiritually and practice unconditional love.

Relationships replay childhood dynamics and unhealed wounds. We tend to bring others into our lives who trigger these replays in an attempt to heal the past. You may remember me mentioning how those closest to us have the ability to push our buttons, now you know why.

If you find yourself experiencing "difficult" relationships, then you have to know that this is down to you and what maybe going on subconsciously. Not a comfortable thought is it?

But think about it for a moment :

Do you have problems with work colleagues generally or one person in particular making life difficult?

Did you experience this in your last place of work as well?

Think about your romantic relationships, why did the last one finish? Have you experienced that before?

What are your expectations in intimate relationships?

Do you expect to be loved and adored or to be let down?

Have you been putting up with "bad behaviour" from those around you?

Is there someone who just annoys you even without doing anything?

Relationships mirror parts of ourselves. We are quite comfortable with the wonderful parts of us we see reflected in others. When we see the "negative" parts reflected, we are often sure it's "the other person's problem!" This is called projection. The stronger your reaction to a "negative" part of someone else, the more likely you are judging some part of yourself. You may also be recalling this behaviour from someone in your childhood.

Your greatest teacher is the person who bothers you the most. So if you find yourself reacting strongly to someone, ask yourself –

"Who does this remind me of?

How old do I feel?

What is it that is really bothering me?"

We all think that if we could just change the other person or get them to see our side then all would be well and we would live happily ever after.

In actual fact it is us that need to make the changes.

We can dramatically improve, heal and resolve conflict by doing the necessary work on ourselves. Following workshops it is wonderful and amazing how many people tell me that problems seemed to have magically dissolved, that difficult or violent people have left their lives or that family rifts are healing.

Once you change your perspective, the way you view yourself and your life, people around you sense that something has fundamentally changed. Even without talking about it the dynamic of the various relationships change and as your thinking becomes more healthy, loving and balanced, anyone in your life who is not that way will no longer feel comfortable with you.

This is alright because you will allow them to leave easily and without the intense pain of separation that you may previously have experienced. As a result more uplifting, healthy and loving relationships will enter your life as you now have space for them.

This has nothing to do with making people like you, or manipulating situations. It has everything to do with you clearing out all negativity and inner beliefs that are attracting less healthy people and experiences into your life.

We have old tape recordings of beliefs and negative messages running through our minds sub-consciously telling us what to expect and how to react. It is a bit like a game of chess. If they do that (move there) then I do this (move here) in order to block or win.

The trouble is it is just that, a game but we get locked into the rules and playing a certain way when it only takes a small change in our outlook, opening up the game plan to let everyone win.

The joy is, right now as you work through this book and the audio exercises you are naturally making the necessary changes on a fundamental level. These changes allow you to heal, move on and bring healthy loving relationships into your life.

Stop the criticism and judgement of others.

Experience has taught me that you cannot always see the hurt or burden that someone is carrying. A lot of people are fearful and this is expressed in the way they deal with others. Look past the façade. When you are interacting with others allow for the fact that they have their own views, issues, fears and passions. They have their own life stories that are unfolding and you have no idea what they are.

No matter how well you know someone never assume that you know what they think or need. You do not. Many wives have complained that their husband has suddenly turned into a stranger or that their secret affair came totally out of the blue and has caused them to behave completely differently. People grow, learn and develop bringing about change almost continuously. What you wanted at 18 you may not want at 30. We are not in a time warp. Relationships need to grow and develop or can become stifling.

Remember also that we all make mistakes as we live and grow. If you are in a any kind of relationship it is important to clear out and let things go, dealing with them at the appropriate time rather than storing them up and spitting them back at someone when you get into an argument.

The Law of Attraction (What you Give out you get Back)

If you are fearful, angry or critical you will find yourself attracting experiences which bring this out in others. If you criticise others then you will be criticised. Likewise if you are criticising yourself internally and possibly sub-consciously, then again you will attract criticism from others.

Whilst you are practising self love you will find an increasing amount of love in your life. Life will be smoother and happier.

I keep mentioning this universal law which many have written about that says what you focus on grows, what you think about most you will attract. If your thoughts are predominantly negative then those are the experiences you will continue to attract. Conversely if your thoughts are positive then that is what you will attract.

Maybe you can remember a time when you were on a high. You may have just been asked out on a date by someone you fancied for ages. You may have just been given a promotion or passed an exam. If you think back to that time you may also remember how around then you hit a "golden period" where everything seemed to go your way. You felt attractive, were happy with your weight, felt like the world was your oyster. All of that will have been brought about by your thoughts at the time. With the positive events came more positive thoughts and experiences. This will have continued until something seemingly "burst your bubble" or in reality negative thoughts took hold again.

Some of you may have noticed that whilst you did not have an intimate relationship no dates were coming your way. Once you broke out of that scenario and got involved suddenly "like buses" it seemed like every person you met was interested in dating you. It is the thought and vibrational pattern that we give out that makes that happen. This is also reflected in your body language. We are either open to good experiences or closed and limited in the belief that nothing good comes to us. Likewise we come from a place of love or a place of fear and I will discuss that further later.

That is why it is so important to make positive affirmations such as "I have loving, harmonious relationships" or "I encounter friendship wherever I go". If you dislike those around you and continue thinking that way, you will bring more of the same. Even if you have a new relationship or move house you will find that you are yet again surrounded by people you dislike.

Think in terms of radio waves, what you give out you get back. You are sending out signals all the time about how you feel and what you believe. The signal goes out and is reflected back at you in your life experience. If you wanted to listen to Radio 1 (British pop music station) it would be no good tuning into Radio 5 (current affairs) it may prove interesting for a while but it is not what you wanted so you would change channels.

You cannot see the radio waves you may not understand how it all works but you take it for granted that it does. It is the same with your own thoughts. You give out signals and those who are tuning into that kind of signal will listen and be attracted to you. If you want to change your experiences then change the signal you give out – change your thoughts.

If you have found yourself in relationships that all seem to turn out the same way then this is confirmation that you are sending out messages that match that experience. It then becomes "the chicken and egg argument" your experiences lead you to think "relationships always turn out badly for me" and this is then confirmed in the next relationship, so the thought continues and the experiences match.

Yes it is YOU and your thoughts and beliefs that create this circle of events!

I have met many women who saw themselves as "victims", some had abusive relationships others feared any relationship. They all had past experiences or ingrained beliefs from what they saw or were told whilst growing up that caused them to be this way. As adults they were choosing to stay that way by not reviewing what had been going on in their relationships and their own part in it.

I was fascinated when a man who had been an abuser attended my workshop. He had stopped having intimate relationships because he did not want to abuse women and yet this seemed to be a pattern. As a child his father had violently abused his mother and he had often tried to protect her from him. So he was mortified that he behaved like his father.

He came to the workshop to deal with this. He shared with the group how after extricating himself from an unhealthy relationship he had gone out to a night club with his male friends. They were all single guys and were "on the pull" as they say, looking for female company. He told them he was just going to sit at the bar and have a drink but would not be getting involved with any girls that night (he had already realised the ones he picked always repeated a pattern and no longer trusted his own judgement). He was only at the bar a short time when a woman stood next to him and actually chatted him up. He was delighted as he thought this would bring a fresh experience…she chose him this time. They got on very well but a little later he was devastated to find she had been involved in an abusive relationship and her previous partner had been violent. This finally made him realise that Victim and abuser are all part of the same game plan. Both are attracted to each other by the sub conscious signals they give out.

This works with everything and anything so it is important to become aware of your thoughts and live more consciously.

Parents/Family

Many of us have this image of an ideal family with an abundance of love readily expressed and felt, in a warm family home. The reality can be very different.

If you have an issue with either of your parents remember that they were a product of their childhood upbringing. It is very hard to be a loving parent if you were not loved as a child or did not see love expressed within the family.

If you have the opportunity to talk with your parents ask them about their childhood (remember to keep this conversation open and non-judgmental) you may find that it gives you a great deal of insight and you may gain a new perspective on them and your own childhood.

In my workshops we cover how the effects of our parents and the messages we learned as we grew up impact our adult lives and in particular relationships. This occurs until we learn new ways and reassess what we learned growing up.

Whilst I advocate "dealing with your stuff" and clearing out any old hurts, anger, resentment or any other emotions that you may be holding with regard to your parents I do not support confronting them with issues. Whilst you may have been working on your "stuff" they may not have been working on theirs and may have no idea what you are talking about. If one or both of your parents have violent tendencies then any sort of confrontation will be a risk.

Once you have done the clearing, releasing and healing work necessary on yourself you will find that all your relationships change around you and confrontation is not required or desirable.

The Inner Child and Healing Old Wounds

Working with your own inner child can assist the process of healing from that longing for parental approval, attention or love. No matter what our age, inside we all have a little child. This little person can hold the key to why you feel the way you do about things, and you become aware of their presence sometimes when you feel sad or a seemingly "irrational" fear shows itself and you find yourself behaving or reacting in an extreme way to something ,or someone for no apparent reason. Using various techniques you can get back in touch with your little person and heal any old hurts or traumas you may have experienced. You will find more on this later in the book.

Grief

Is there a process for grief?

Grief is a very personal thing, in my own experience, that gleaned from research and listening to others. No two people grieve in the same way although there may be similarities.

Those who specialise in grief counselling will tell you that it goes through specific phases - denial, anger, sadness, bargaining and acceptance. I have never liked any sort of prescriptive statement of an emotional process like this. Whenever people encounter it whilst grieving they invariably try to work out what part of the process they are in and if they fit the "norm".

When people ask - "Will it get better/easier?" the general answer is yes but there will likely always be a part of us that still grieves if only a little, we mainly get on with life and give ourselves over to what we still have in it. There will always be times, depending on the relationship of the person to you, when the loss feels stronger. Family events like Christmas or weddings etc. when they would have played a particular role, been a character, an embarrassment or a rock.

Are you an adult orphan?

Losing the last parent seems to be a slightly different event to the first. Obviously if you lose both parents as a child you are classed as an "orphan" and treated as such. Everyone can instantly sympathise or realise that this is a traumatic event. However, when you are older and your parents die, it sounds ridiculous to say "I am an orphan".

Whilst one parent remains alive you are still a child to someone no matter how old you are and whether or not you have become the carer for that parent. Also you may find that you finally grieve the loss of your first parent, which may not have seemed possible or just may not have happened whilst the other parent was alive. This is sometimes caused by throwing yourself into taking care or being concerned about how the other parent is coping rather than experiencing your own sense of loss.

Once all parents are gone then you are technically an orphan, your position or role has changed. There is a sense of missed opportunities to spend more time together, have that talk, ask those questions. There is also inevitably a feeling of future loss - Mum not seeing your children grow up or even seeing them at all, Dad not seeing you succeed in your field of work or get the award. How are you feeling as you read this section? Just notice.

Illness

Following the death of a loved one we are more prone to infection and illness. It is extremely important to take loving care of yourself. It is well documented that within 12-18months onwards a serious health problem can occur with the long term partner of someone who has died. This reflects the sense of loss of purpose, joy, love of life and negative thoughts and beliefs that can take hold at that time. Being a Carer for an ageing parent can dramatically effect the immune system and scientists have found that their reduced immunity continued even long after they ceased to be Carers.

Guilt

Amongst other feelings and emotions guilt is another one that can be very damaging to your overall health and happiness. No matter what the circumstances most people feel guilty when someone dies. It may be that you feel you did not do enough, did not see them as often as you might, left things unsaid or unresolved. This whole mix can be made very complex if you did not know your parents, felt very antagonistic towards them, in awe or frightened of them.

Freedom

One of the wonderful things that can happen at some point is the realisation that you are free and that a whole new world of opportunities can now open up for you. No matter how wonderful our parents and our childhood, we are still subject to the real or imagined pressure of living the kind of life our parents think we should. Many people have taken courses, jobs, partners, or other things because they believe it makes their parents happy, meets with approval and their expectations and is "the right thing to do".

When both parents die you realise just how much you may have relied, been guided or driven by them in your life even down to everyday decisions. Once they are gone so is the judgement about what you do and you can finally grow up and take your own decisions based totally on what you want and what you think.

When you reach a point where you feel this freedom, use it to motivate you to do all the things that you have always wanted to but felt would not fit with others expectations of you. I am not suggesting you drop all responsibilities (especially if you have children or dependants) but choose to really LIVE your life. Get the most from each day, see the good and the joy in your life in the little and the large things. Do not focus on what is wrong with your life, focus on the good and allow changes to take place in the other areas. Relax this is your life and you are learning techniques here to make it a wonderful life that you love.

There is a book called "Midlife Orphan" by Jane Brooks. It recounts the experiences of others going through this event and the kind of issues that arise. Through its real life stories it is comforting to know that you are not alone and that similar issues come up for others. It also helps you to understand that no matter how long your parents would have lived you probably never would have had the kind of conversation or activities you wish you had. It is also amazing and sad how many family arguments, feuds, rifts go on and can be re-ignited by a death in the family. This need not be true for you now.

If you are experiencing grief, as we all will at sometime in our lives, I am not going to say I understand what you are feeling as I know you are an individual and your experience is unique to you. Losing those close to us is part of life, we have a right to all our feelings and emotions including anger and disappointment.

Make sure you do not remain stuck in the past. Use the releasing and forgiving exercises. Seek out a support group to assist the process of moving forward. Not to forget or negate your feelings but to vent them, allow them to flow out in a healthy way.

Remember you still have a life to experience and fulfil in its richness, gifts to offer, love to share. You carry who ever it is you have lost in a special place in your heart.

Unconditional Love

For many of us the only time we experienced unconditional love is just after we were born. We were fed, cuddled and nurtured even though we threw up, soiled nappies, dribbled and kept others awake when they desperately needed sleep.

Most of us would like to feel so cherished again and for this to happen, as I have stated before, you have to start by loving yourself unconditionally just as you are. Now I would like you to take on board the idea that you can love others in the same way.

Release the need to control your partner/husband/wife/friend and others. Stop judging them against your invisible set of standards. Allow those you love to be all that they can be whether that fits what you want them to be or not. Encourage them and show them love without any expectation of return.

You will find that this act alone, whilst it may seem difficult, takes a lot of pressure off everyone in your relationships especially you. If you get upset every time someone fails to do something in the way or timescale that you want then you are repeatedly going to suffer anger and frustration. As you now know this is to your own detriment.

As part of loving yourself it is right for you to ask others for help and support. However, it is important that just as I have told you to say "no" you accept that they have the right to say "no" also. Bearing a grudge is not loving and as what we give out we get back you can expect the negative thoughts and feelings to come right back at you. Just move on and ask someone else. If you do this with grace you may find the person more likely to help possibly at a more convenient time for them.

So work on losing your "hidden agenda" with regard to lovers, partners, friends and relatives.

Our lives reflect our thoughts.

This is about living consciously. Not only our health and relationships but all aspects of our lives are a reflection of our thoughts.

If you find yourself always short of money, time, love or anything else, then you are probably subject to "poverty thinking". This is a result of thoughts like "there is never enough…", "I want never gets". Most of it we absorbed whilst growing up. Thoughts of lack and limitation bring just that.

We have millions of thoughts continuously and most are sub conscious. They fly by in an instant it is unreasonable to expect you to note them all down and replace the negative thoughts with positive ones.

Most of the thoughts we have today we had yesterday and the day before and the day before………and on and on. We do not need to stay trapped in that limited way of thinking. We can actively introduce new positive thoughts to create a more healthy, happy tomorrow. You can also use your "internal guidance system" to alert you to negative thought patterns as they are occurring.

You may have noticed that when your thoughts are negative your body feels very uncomfortable and this you can use to your advantage whilst making changes. Generally the feelings are linked to love or fear.

So, are YOU coming from a place of Love or Fear?

At any given moment, you are either coming from a place of love or a place of fear. When you come from a place of love then any decisions you make are generally good. You know they are choices and if they do not work out then you can choose again. Whereas, when you come from a place of fear you are attempting to manipulate or control a situation in order to minimise your risk. We sometimes jump ahead in our thinking because of previous experience and assume the worst in a situation.

An easy place to see us not being authentic and coming from a place of fear is when we first start a relationship. As women, we dress with a great deal of thought and behave in the way we think makes us most adorable. If asked to a football match when we hate football we will probably say "yes" as the thought "if I don't he may take it the wrong way or decide that I am not for him or not interested in him". So we go and hate it, but are happy to be with him. As time goes by and the relationship develops we do not admit we lied and keep going along to the matches, sometimes with gritted teeth and forced smiles. This builds up within us and becomes resentment. When it finally bursts out, possibly during a row, the person is hurt and suddenly starts to wonder what else you lied about and if he really knows you at all. Now, whilst I used women in this example the same is also true for men.

At work, you can put yourself through hell, as in for instance expecting to have an interview with your boss later that day. You spend the whole day worrying about what will be discussed, are you next on the redundancy list? Are you getting fired? As you now know "what you focus on grows" so this line of thought is going nowhere good. By the time the interview comes you are exhausted and feel defeated, defensive or angry.

Many children might tell you that their mother has said "you wait till your father gets home" in such a tone and in such a way that they have spent the rest of the day in constant stress and fear of what is to come. They remember another time when Dad told them off or punished them. Later their father arrives home, mum has forgotten all about it and nothing happens, but the child has spent a day in fear and this will continue through the night until they are sure that the threat is over. They would prefer it if Dad would come and tell them off or give them a punishment so that it is over and done with.

In many ways you are doing the same thing and it is not always resolved.

The chances are most of the fear comes from childhood, it can relate to fear of not being good enough, being left/abandoned, not having enough, or just not being lovable.

Work quite often conflicts with social and family activities. Again if you are coming from a place of fear then you will stay late, write the extra report or miss the party or school play. Because you want to keep your job, be a good employee, prove you can cope, not let your boss down. As time goes on you will notice that it is always you who gets asked to do the extra work.

Most life coaches at this point work on prioritising your life and goals and organising your time. However, no matter how well organised you are there will always be times when those plans go awry. So what then?

Use your Internal Guidance System

What I want you to do is start to recognise your own internal barometer or guidance system. Each time a decision comes up, notice how your body feels. If it feels uncomfortable with what you are about to do or say then consider alternatives and notice if your body feels any different.

By now you are putting yourself first (extreme self care) and your body will respond to whether you are following that pattern or not. You will naturally and automatically have your boundaries and these will be picked up by those around you. You will trust your own judgement rather than looking for guidance or approval from others and as your love and trust for yourself grows you will not hurt yourself or anyone else. You will feel more relaxed.

So from now on when someone comes and asks you to do something or a situation where you have to make a choice arises I want you to:-

take a breath, ask yourself "am I coming from a place of love or a place of fear?"

Before you answer or decide, use the way your body feels as a guide.

If the answer is a place of love then your body will feel comfortable and you can go ahead and make that choice.

If not then wait until you have thought through what you would like to do (or your body would feel more comfortable with) then make your choice.

Remember there is always choice. The reason we do not always see that, is because we get trapped in negative thought patterns and situations. We deny our personal power and then the fear takes over.

As long as we live we always have a chance to do things differently. Each morning when you awaken you can choose how you will feel about the day. If you do not like the way your life looks then change it and start by changing the way you feel about it. As we discussed before what you focus on grows. If you spend your days thinking how awful life is for you then guess what? It will stay that way.

Use your inner barometer to monitor how you are feeling at any given time and if it feels bad then change your thoughts and adjust what you are doing as whatever you are thinking and doing are not taking you anywhere good.

Monitoring yourself can be very challenging initially as we are not aware of all of our thoughts and there are so many flooding in. We don't always remember to check in with ourselves to see how we are feeling. However, as you enter each part of your day turn to thoughts that fit the current activity and make them positive.

An Example – going to work:

Whilst finishing your breakfast you would set your intention for the day. This might be to have an effective yet relaxed day and for all interactions with others to be positive, productive and harmonious. *(As you get practiced at this you would start with affirmations about having a great day as soon as you wake up)*.

You are about to leave for work so before you get into your car, you think ahead and visualise a safe journey with the perfect parking space ready for you as you arrive. Then you relax.

As you park the car you are about to start a new activity so as you enter the office pre-pave your way again with thoughts of a happy effective day and the attendant feelings this would bring. It needs to be done in a relaxed way but with the certainty that you are setting the stage for a more positive experience.

Give this a try you will be amazed at the difference it will make relatively quickly if you give it a good go.

Taking this a stage further, it is also very important to be honest and practise unconditional love.

Honesty

In your general approach to all things be honest. It is amazing how much time we spend making up excuses for why we cannot do things, be or have what we want. Sometimes it seems to spiral out of control.

Once you start coming from a place of love rather than fear, you will find it increasingly difficult to lie. This is a good thing, you no longer have hidden agendas and it makes you more comfortable to be around.

Honesty extends to all aspects of your life.

The saying "if you take from life then life will take from you" or "what goes around comes around" are relevant here. By now you are already practising daily positive affirmations and coming from a place of love. Being honest with yourself is extremely important and now you must extend this honesty to others.

If you work in an office you may not feel the honesty extends to inanimate objects or a large corporation. In your daily life you may feel that shops or banks are fair game and if they make an error then it is OK for you to take advantage of it.

From taking paper clips out of the office, being undercharged in a shop or given too much change, to undertaking a burglary, these are all stealing. Whether it is a large business or a little old Lady that you are cheating, makes no difference. It makes a clear statement of "I have to get my good by taking it from someone else". That is coming from a place of fear. As what we give out we get back, you can expect that if good things come to you they will very soon be taken from you too.

The really amazing thing is that once you adopt a policy of absolute honesty it really pays off in your favour. It has become so much a part of my nature now that if I suspect that I have not paid enough or that there is an error I have to bring it to the others attention (it is worth remembering that shop assistants can be sacked if their till is short). Ever since I adopted this policy I have lost count of the times I have been given extra bonuses with my purchase or the price of the item I am buying has been cut that very morning. I regularly pay less than I expect.

I trust myself, I trust others and I always affirm that everything I want is at a price I can easily afford. It sounds strange I know but it works really well.

SUMMARY

Have a good clear out. Whether it is just one drawer or a room, do it now.

Consider the relationships you have with those around you. What are they mirroring back to you?
What would you like to have mirrored back to you?
Have you noticed any changes lately in the way people relate to you?

Practise unconditional love with yourself and others. Ditch the hidden agenda.

Use your internal guidance system. Before making an important decision always check your body for signs that all is not well. If you are entirely comfortable then it is a good decision.

Honesty really is the best policy in all things.

Set your intention at the beginning of each day for what you want to experience. Use affirmations and visualisation as you move from one activity to another and then relax.

Your Inner Child

All of us have an inner child or even inner children of various ages. Your inner child may be perfectly happy, but could also be frightened, shy, hurt, upset, angry or feeling unloved.

These normally reflect us at various key stages in our development. If something happens or has a big impact on us at these stages then it gets locked away and the child stays in that position/emotion within us. It has an effect on our current judgements and decisions even though we are totally unaware of it.

Guided meditations are very useful in trying to get back in touch with our inner child, we will do a meditation exercise from your *Release & Heal CD* shortly.

When you make contact you may feel sadness or confusion. Stick with it this is a good thing. You are building trust here. So when you first get to see them in a meditation just show them love and gratitude for showing up.

As the trust builds they will share things with you. The important thing at this point is to keep meditating regularly so that you can keep in contact. This is another one of those instances where you have to trust in the process even though it may sound alien to you.

To give you some examples from people I have seen:

One lady got to see a child in her meditation who did not say anything and seemed sad, continuously looking over her shoulder. As this lady kept meditating and the trust grew, the child shared her fears and the reason she was looking over her shoulder.
This lady came from a family with a history of abuse.
She was able to make this child feel loved and safe.
You see as I have mentioned before, you will never leave yourself, you will always be there and you can provide the kind of comfort, love and support that no one else ever could. As this contact developed issues with her weight diminished and healing started to take place. Weight quite often represents fear or safety issues and a need for a barrier to keep people away.

Following on with the theme of weight –

another lady who was having issues in her current relationship and had always experienced fluctuations in her weight suddenly reconnected with her 11 – 13 year old inner child. This child felt ugly and fat with glasses, she could not compete with her beautiful, thin sister.
This child had built barriers believing herself to be unlovable, her experiences reflected this. Even though none of this was true that child was still having an effect on her adult behaviour today. The body accommodates our belief system so as she believed she was fat and ugly the body set about matching her belief. No diet would be effective until that core belief had been changed and she could visualise herself as beautiful and the perfect weight for her. Extra work with the inner child through guided meditation healed that part of her life.

The importance of the connection -

A gentleman, following an inner child meditation with me had the urge to walk on the beach, he followed through on this and felt such a flood of love and gratitude inside that he is now totally hooked on meditating, listening and acting upon the messages that come from it.

127

This leads me onto a very important point to remember. If either during or after a meditation of this nature you have a very strong desire to do something (as long as it is not illegal or dangerous) then do it. This is a desire coming from your inner child or sub conscious and if you act on it then a direct message that you have heard goes to your child or sub conscious. This builds trust in the connection and you will find more and more insight on what makes you happy coming through.

A word of caution, in the same way as acting on such messages or feelings builds trust and the connection, ignoring them has the opposite effect and the connection will be broken.

When you make contact with your inner child, take particular note (write down afterwards) what your child is doing, holding, playing, looking like etc. Eventually they may speak or show you something. No matter what it is, whether it makes sense to you or not remember it. The significance of it may come later.

Exercise 16 – Audio Inner Child Meditation

Use the Inner Child Meditation on your *Release & Heal CD*, track 8.

Alternatively - Get your drawing pad and crayons out again.

Refer back to the previous non-dominant hand drawing exercise, this time do your own meditation and visualise a child playing in the park and coming up to you. Imagine that this child is you at the age of 5 or 6, ask her some questions but if she does not seem to talk to you then notice how she looks, if she is carrying anything in her hands etc.

When you open your eyes, with your non-dominant hand draw whatever comes to you.

"Professional" Guidance
Where and when

If you know you have been abused in the past, suffered some kind of trauma, are experiencing depression or abuse of any kind currently - then you need professional help. They will guide you through the process of releasing and clearing in a safe and positive way at a pace that is right for you.

If you are getting very strong reactions or resistance to what you have been reading or doing here then the time has come to find yourself a practitioner to assist you.

When choosing a professional/practitioner consider the following:

- Qualifications & insurance

- Recommendations are worth following up

- Safe space, location, surroundings, will you be alone etc.

- Speak with them first on the telephone or if possible pop down to their office for a quick non-committal chat.

- Be clear about the process they use and what it will entail

- If you do not feel comfortable with them then do not make an appointment

- Trust your own judgement, if what they say does not make sense to you then walk away

- Do not feel pressured to sign up for long periods of time.

- Be prepared to make time for appointments no matter how busy you are and then stick with them

- If you do not feel or see benefits then stop

Why go on a Workshop?

There are many workshops and courses that you can attend using various techniques physical, emotional and mental to assist you on your path. So you can pick one that fits your particular needs. The joy of attending group sessions like these is that you are with a group of
likeminded people. You can learn from the experiences of the others attending as well as the teacher and you can acquire new skills at a fairly gentle pace under supervision.
The tendency can be to take things a little too seriously and become a little too introverted when we start doing work on ourselves. When working with a group this is less likely to happen and can bring some of the fun and humour back.

You need to go with an open mind. If it feels right for you, you are free at that time and can afford it, then it is right for you. However, you are still an adult and free thinker if you do not like what is going on or it sounds too off base for you then it probably is and you should give it a miss.

Use one day sessions and short courses as tasters for particular therapies and disciplines. If it works for you then you might consider booking one to one sessions with the practitioner.

When choosing a workshop:

Most of the above rules for choosing a professional apply here too.

Ask as many questions before booking as you like, you need to know this is right for you.

When attending a workshop:

You have taken time out, invested money and energy in this activity so take an active part. This is your opportunity to do things under guidance that you may not be able to do alone. However, use your own judgement as to whether or not something is appropriate for you.

Sometimes it is a good idea to go to another area completely or book into a hotel, just so that you are dedicating your time to the process.

Be unavailable to others (friends, relatives) for the entire workshop period.

I run several workshops throughout the year, every year in the UK and abroad. I also hold private workshops and one to one sessions and a Teacher Training Programme. For more information visit www.aplacefortheheart.co.uk

A Change in Focus

What do you really want?

I hope you are beginning to understand that a world of infinite possibilities is opening up for you. Your life may already be exactly what you want and that is wonderful. Some of it might be good, whilst other parts not so good. I want you to start expanding your thinking in terms of what kind of life you want to create.

Sometimes when you work on yourself as you have been doing, you remember dreams you used to have, gifts and talents you never used or developed further. Maybe now is the time to dust off some of those. Leave the "oh, but I can't because…." out of this. Just allow yourself to start day dreaming about how your life might be.

It is surprising that when you ask most people what they really want in their lives they normally start with what they don't want. If put on a spot generally people opt for lots of money, a better job, a bigger house or car. Once you get past that and ask what kind of job, doing what, where and how? What size house, location, circumstances and amenities do you want, and so on. The answers to these questions are things like, "not the job I am doing now, something better"; "not my house something bigger and better".

If you do not know what you want how can you expect the universe to bring it to you or your subconscious and higher self to be able to achieve the goal?

It is important that you affirm for the things you want in your life. Remember the *Law of attraction* "**What you focus on grows**".

In going for perfect health you don't affirm "I don't want bad health anymore" you state "I have perfect health".

However, as I know most people focus on the negatives in the beginning I am asking you right now to use each activity, every day as a guide for collecting information on what you want. So when you get up in the morning feeling tired you know that you want to awaken feeling refreshed and bright. As you go to work perhaps on the train you may think "I want a great car" and you might take that further by thinking through what colour you would like. If you see a car you like then you say "that's for me!"

If you see something you do not like then you turn your attention elsewhere.

The important thing is to focus on and give positive thought only to what you want. To take that a stage further add as much detail to it as you can and picture it.

Another good way to focus is to start by going on a retreat for the soul. Giving yourself time off to do something you love. Firstly you have to work out what form this retreat will take. See the next exercise.

Exercise 17 - Retreat for the Soul

It is very important to schedule time for yourself to contemplate particular issues, life changes or just to have "down" time to rest and recuperate. These times are best spent alone. If you must have company go on an organised retreat where there will be other likeminded individuals and arrange it so that you get to spend some time alone.

Make sure you set a date and clear the space in your diary. Once you have found a space then complete the following in your notebook:-

The retreat for my soul is scheduled for:

To do this I need to (e.g. clear my desk, book holiday time from work, get someone to feed the dog):

The place/places I would most like to go are (e.g. somewhere you have always wanted to visit):

I'd like to use this retreat to (e.g. nourish myself spiritually and emotionally, learn a new skill, bring out my creative side):

Exercise 18 - Visualise a Dream

Sit quietly and visualise something you would like to happen. First time make it simple but add as much detail as you can.

So if for instance I was looking for more friends in my life, I would visualise myself as a loving, friendly and outgoing person surrounded by uplifting fun people. I would feel the emotions and feelings that would evoke in me i.e. happy, relaxed, having fun.

I would repeat this visualisation until it felt believable and then I would release it by putting my visualisation in a pink bubble and releasing it into the ether. Watching it drift away with no fear or worry or attachment to it at all, trusting that it will return to me in the "real" world when the time is right.

Whilst in the relaxed meditative state I would also use affirmations.

Gentle Reminder

Just be willing - The thing about all these techniques is to be in a position and of a mind to give them a fair chance.

Exercise 19 - Creating a Happy, Healthy Future

This is a guided meditation on your *Release & Heal CD*, track 9.

A Lovely Side Effect

Something I have noticed through doing workshops is that participants especially the female ones often look younger afterwards.

When you take away the intense need for approval, the burden of carrying loads for others, and the desperate need for love and fulfilment, you see the person relax and become spontaneous. This allows the facial muscles to relax and expression lines soften.

This is what one lady wrote to me after a workshop *"I can't thank you enough Gillian. I actually wake up in the mornings looking forward to the day ahead! I feel great, even my mum said I look like a thirty year old with a spring in my step. It's Great! (oh by the way I am 50 next month, I really don't feel it now). It is amazing how loving yourself can change so many things ".*

Dale Carnegie describes the same process when he talks of people who have been reborn and found the love of God he calls it "Gods' Beauty Parlour" as the difference can be quite striking.

Decide now that you are worth loving and that you are going to take the time and necessary steps to love yourself. Accept yourself and love yourself as you are today. Quite often we feel that we will be more lovable when we are thinner, richer, more successful, better dressed etc. We all have parts of ourselves that we do not like, be they physical attributes or personality traits. Denying them or cutting them off from us creates stress and disease within the body.

As far as the dark sides of our nature are concerned if you shut them away in a dark room then they always have the potential to frighten you or appear at inappropriate moments. Whereas if you shine the light on them, like shadows, they disappear and become reintegrated into our whole selves in a healthy way.

If you want changes to take place in your life on all levels then you need to start now as you are. Once you truly feel accepted and loved as you are you will find it easy to make changes, in fact the changes will take place naturally by themselves as you will be working with and not against yourself.

This is all about getting back in touch with your authentic self. The you that came into this world full of love and hope, fascinated by life and the world around you and happy just looking at your toes!

 # Practical Activity Summary

- Commit to change.

- Set aside certain times to undertake this work at a pace to suit you and stick with it.

- Review your life to date, be honest with yourself and celebrate your successes.

- Start treating yourself as you would a loving child who is learning something new.

- Give your body the premium fuel it needs.

- Use Yoga, Pilates, a favourite sport, or just walking to improve your circulation, body tone, breathing and the mind/body connection.

- Start the day with positive affirmations.

- List your favourite activities/indulgences, do one of them today and another by the end of the week. Now build these things regularly into your schedule.

- Accept help graciously when it is offered. Only offer help when you are genuinely happy to give it.

- Understand that making mistakes or slipping back a little is part of human nature and can also be a positive sign. Do not beat yourself up over it. Continue with your positive work.

- Do not try to make loads of changes to yourself. When you get to your heart centre and love and accept yourself as you are, these changes will happen naturally and easily.

- If you have people in your life who drain you and make you feel depressed stay clear of them or if this is not possible whilst in this process reduce your exposure to them. Stop taking those late night telephone calls.

- Avoid watching the news, heavy documentaries or violent films before going to bed. This will only focus your attention on the negativity in the world and will not make for a good nights sleep.

- Accept yourself exactly as you are, allowing yourself to relax and the changes to happen naturally.

- Forgive everyone especially yourself, release all guilt, anger, resentment and fear.

- Make choices from love not fear.

- Write in your gratitude journal every night and follow with the "Loving Treatment".

- Work with your inner child to make them feel safe and loved.

- Open your heart and allow the love to flow and watch it return to you multiplied

I trust that before reading this part you have worked through all the exercises and tried the techniques I have given you. If not, why not? Could there be some resistance to doing this, some fear of opening up and letting out whatever it is that has created your health problems?

Whatever your current situation I urge you as one human being to another to give this a try, you will learn so much about yourself. If it all feels like too much to do alone then get to a workshop or local practitioner and let others help you through.

For those of you who have worked your way through, congratulations you are opening up a whole new world for yourself. Keep practising, keep clearing and keep coming from a loving place in your heart. You have started a particular process in motion, you already feel that happening, changes may be coming quickly and it can seem a little scary. In your heart you know this is what needs to happen and you have been waiting a long time for this. Stick with it and keep affirming:

"everything is working out perfectly".

If you now remain true to your feelings and emotions and what is best for you, it will bring wonderful changes not only for you but those around you.

Resources

Workshops & Teacher Training

Gillian runs several group and private workshops each year in the UK and abroad as well as a Teacher Training Programme. If you would like to attend a workshop then having purchased this book you will receive a £25 discount on the regular price. It is an amazing experience and you can read testimonials and get further details from the website www.aplacefortheheart.co.uk alternatively write to me at the address given below.

Heal Your Life CD

This CD incorporates the doors and anger meditation and chant that you experience on the "Release & Heal" CD accompanying this book plus another chant and meditation. In addition there are chants with quiet music so that you can do your own meditations.

Heartfelt Affirmations to Release the Past CD

A very useful CD for assisting the process of release and it also incorporates an "Affirmation Bath" normally only available in group workshops. I have reproduced the affects of an affirmation bath on the "Heartfelt" CD to assist the "opening up to receiving more love" process.

Songs for the Inner Child CD – Shaina Noll

This is a great CD to use whilst doing any kind of inner child work. The songs seem to touch your heart and can assist the release of emotion.

For further information on any of the above products visit www.aplacefortheheart.co.uk or write to Gillian Bowles, PO Box 132, Penarth, Vale of Glamorgan CF64 2YY.

Recommended Sites

A Place for the Heart
For those seeking inspiration and emotional healing at all levels. Details of workshops, teacher training, products, free resources and one to one sessions with Gillian.
www.aplacefortheheart.co.uk

The Positive Mindset Website
Affirmation site offering information on using positive thinking techniques to live a more fulfilled life. Explore the Healing Cards!
www.vitalaffirmations.com

The Cosmic Ordering Site
Place your cosmic order now to manifest your dreams.
www.thecosmicorderingsite.com

Angel Message 4 You
A small site that offers a free "Angel Message" to its visitors, great for receiving a little extra guidance.
www.angelmessage4u.com

Natural Facelift Method
We are all beautiful but sometimes as we get a little older we need some help to maintain our outer beauty.
 www.facelift4u.com

NOTES